RAMOS

MATT AND TOM OLDFIELD

ULTIMATE FOOTBALL HEROES

RAMOS

FROM THE PLAYGROUND TO THE PITCH

DINO

First published by Dino Books in 2019,
an imprint of Bonnier Books UK,
The Plaza,
535 Kings Road,
London SW10 0SZ

🔲 @dinobooks
🔲 @footieheroesbks
www.heroesfootball.com
www.bonnierbooks.co.uk

Design and typesetting by www.envydesign.co.uk

Paperback ISBN: 978 1 78946 118 3
E-book ISBN: 978 1 78946 181 7

British Library Cataloguing-in-Publication Data:
A catalogue record for this book is available from the British Library.

Printed and bound in Great Britain by Clays Ltd, Elcograf S.p.A.

1 3 5 7 9 10 8 6 4 2

For all readers,
young and old(er)

ULTIMATE FOOTBALL HEROES

Matt Oldfield is an accomplished writer and the editor-in-chief of football review site *Of Pitch & Page*. Tom Oldfield is a freelance sports writer and the author of biographies on Cristiano Ronaldo, Arsène Wenger and Rafael Nadal.

Cover illustration by Dan Leydon.
To learn more about Dan visit danleydon.com
To purchase his artwork visit etsy.com/shop/footynews
Or just follow him on Twitter @danleydon

TABLE OF CONTENTS

ACKNOWLEDGEMENTS

First of all, I'd like to thank Bonnier Books UK – and particularly my editor Laura Pollard – for supporting me throughout and running the ever-expanding UFH ship so smoothly. Writing stories for the next generation of football fans is both an honour and a pleasure.

I wouldn't be doing this if it wasn't for my brother Tom. I owe him so much and I'm very grateful for his belief in me as an author. I feel like Robin setting out on a solo career after a great partnership with Batman. I hope I do him (Tom, not Batman) justice with these new books.

Next up, I want to thank my friends for keeping

me sane during long hours in front of the laptop. Pang, Will, Mills, Doug, John, Charlie – the laughs and the cups of coffee are always appreciated.

I've already thanked my brother but I'm also very grateful to the rest of my family, especially Melissa, Noah and of course Mum and Dad. To my parents, I owe my biggest passions: football and books. They're a real inspiration for everything I do.

Finally, I couldn't have done this without Iona's encouragement and understanding during long, work-filled weekends. Much love to you.

CHAPTER 1

KING OF EUROPE

26 May 2018, NSC Olimpiyskiy Stadium, Kiev

As the referee blew the final whistle, Sergio dropped
to his knees and threw his arms in the air. Real
Madrid were once again the Kings of Europe and,
as the team captain, he was just minutes away
from lifting the Champions League trophy in front
of thousands of joyful fans. Before he could finish
that thought, he was wrapped in hugs from his
teammates.

Campeones, Campeones, Olé, Olé, Olé!

On TV screens around the world, millions of fans
watched on. 'It's another magical night to be a Real

Madrid fan,' the commentator announced excitedly. 'Zinedine Zidane continues to get the best out of this team and they have match-winners all over the pitch as we saw tonight – Cristiano Ronaldo, Gareth Bale, Karim Benzema, Luka Modrić and on and on.'

Sergio grinned as he looked around the stadium. He would be enjoying a Champions League victory lap for the fourth time, but the feeling never got old. 'Wooooo!' he said, high-fiving Luka. 'We weren't at our best, but we found a way! Now let's get the party started.'

The cameras were flocking towards Gareth, who had been the difference-maker with two second-half goals, including a spectacular bicycle kick. Meanwhile, Sergio jogged over to congratulate his manager, putting his arm round Zinedine as they waved to the thousands of Real Madrid fans in the crowd.

'Zizou, you're making life as a manager look pretty easy!' Sergio shouted, just loud enough to be heard over the cheers.

Zinedine smiled and shrugged. 'What can I say? You guys make me look good.'

It had been an emotional night for Sergio, who had tangled with Liverpool's Mo Salah in the first half. After the Egyptian had to go off with a shoulder injury, the Liverpool fans starting booing loudly every time Sergio touched the ball.

Fouler! Cheat!

Sergio was used to making enemies on the football pitch, however. He loved the physical battles between defender and striker. There were often yellow and red cards along the way, but he almost always won the fight. And in the biggest games of all, like the Champions League Final, the Real Madrid captain was unbeatable.

As Sergio was joining in the dancing and singing with his teammates, a fan passed Sergio a Spanish flag and he wrapped it round his shoulders. They had been through some tough tests together, but that had only made their bond stronger.

'Can you believe we've won three Champions League titles in a row?' Karim called. 'No-one can say we're not the best team in the world now!'

Sergio could see the UEFA staff setting up the

stage for the trophy presentation, with people rushing around and security guards making sure there was a safe space for the players. A man in a smart suit was talking to some of the Real Madrid coaches and pointing to the left-hand side of the stage. It was trophy time!

Sergio knew the drill by now. He drifted towards the back of the line. The captain always stood last so he was in the right place to receive the trophy. He waited patiently as his teammates stepped forward in turn, shook hands and got their medals – each taking a moment to admire the shiny design.

By the time it was finally Sergio's turn, his teammates were already singing and jumping, arms around each other. He grinned. It was impossible not to. It was an incredible feeling to get the winners' medal that they had all worked so hard for, but it was nothing compared to being the first one of them to get his hands on the trophy.

Once he had received his medal, Sergio turned to his teammates. 'Ready, boys?'

They cheered and sang even louder.

Sergio reached forward and firmly gripped both handles of the trophy. The last thing he wanted was to be seen in videos all over the Internet dropping it! He lifted the trophy, gave it one quick kiss and then raised it high above his head.

'Vamooooooooos!' he yelled.

It was one of those nights when Sergio just didn't want to leave the pitch. He could still see lots of Real Madrid fans in the crowd, savouring every moment. He clapped and waved again.

At last, it was time to take the party back to the dressing room and then to a special event at their hotel with friends and family. He couldn't wait to see his wife, Pilar, and his kids, Sergio Jr., Marco and Alejandro.

Sergio took one last look at the stadium – the confetti still scattered across the ground, the white shirts and scarves in the crowd, and the happy faces everywhere. He closed his eyes and smiled.

He still had to pinch himself at times to be sure he wasn't dreaming. The celebrations could wait an extra minute or two, he decided. He leaned against the dugout on the far side of the pitch and allowed himself to think back to his hometown of Camas where it had all begun – before the Champions League titles, before conquering the world with Spain, before signing with Real Madrid in the Galácticos era. It had been quite a journey – and it wasn't over yet.

CHAPTER 2

OLYMPIC INSPIRATION

'The game is about to start!' little Sergio called, scampering into the kitchen, before rushing back into the living room.

He jumped up onto the sofa and sat in his favourite spot – the one with the best view of the TV. It was past his bedtime, but his parents knew that there was no chance of him falling asleep anyway. School was finished for the summer and the rules had been relaxed.

'So, are you still feeling confident?' his dad, José María, asked him. 'You really think Spain can win the gold?'

The 1992 Olympic Games were being held in

Barcelona, and it was all anyone could talk about. Sergio had been telling everyone for weeks that the Spanish football team was destined to do well.

'Of course!' he replied. 'Our team is great – Kiko, Pep Guardiola, Luis Enrique… *and* we're playing at home. You just wait and see!'

'Sergio knows his stuff,' his mum, Paqui, added. 'Who knows – maybe one day that'll be you out there playing for Spain!'

Sergio loved that idea, but for now, he was ready to cheer on his national heroes in their opening match against Colombia. Within minutes, he was running through the living room as Guardiola put Spain ahead.

Goooooooooooooooooooooaaaaaaaaaaaaaaaalllllllllllll llllllllllllll!!!!!!!!!!!!!!!!!!!

By now, René, his older brother, had joined the party. They high-fived and sat side-by-side on the sofa. His sister, Miriam, perched on the armrest.

Spain were already ahead of Colombia by 3–0 at half-time and Sergio could just sit back and enjoy the game. He loved how the Spanish players passed the ball so effortlessly around the pitch, waiting for the right moment to pounce. They were off to the perfect start.

That night, Sergio lay on his bed holding his favourite football, which was scuffed and slightly ripped from many hours of use. He threw it into the air and caught it again. How was he meant to sleep after watching that game? He wanted to be outside, pretending that he played for Spain!

The next afternoon, he dribbled that same ball to the park with his friends, Felix and Fernando. Like him, all they wanted to talk about was Spain's chances of winning the gold medal. They set up a goal with two jumpers and took turns pretending to be Luis Enrique.

'Cross it in!' Sergio called out as Felix dribbled forward. Every time one of them scored, they recreated the goal celebrations they had watched the night before.

By the end of the group stage, Sergio's prediction was starting to look good. Spain finished top of their group, then sneaked through to the semi-finals.

Sergio had been biting his nails throughout the quarter-final, but Paqui decided it was not the time to make a comment to her son.

As Spain kept winning, Sergio was more and more glued to the action. José María could only smile – his youngest child had shown a flicker of interest in football before that summer, but now it was all he thought about.

'We can't miss the game,' Sergio pleaded on the day of the semi-final against Ghana as the family left the house for a picnic. 'I'm their lucky charm!'

'Don't worry,' José María said, laughing. 'We'll be back in plenty of time for you to change into your lucky shirt, get a drink in your lucky cup and sit at your lucky end of the sofa.'

Sergio smiled. 'Sorry, just checking.'

The Ramos house had a Spanish flag in the window along with all the different red and yellow decorations that were being given out all over the country for the Olympics. As promised, they were all back from their picnic well before kick-off and Sergio had time to watch all the pre-game build-up.

He joined in with the national anthem and then silence fell over the whole house as the game began. Even through the TV, Sergio could hear the crowd roaring for Spain to make a good start – and they did, with Abelardo, a defender, scoring.

'Yes!' Sergio clapped his hands and jumped up off the sofa.

'See, Sergio, defenders can still score goals,' José María teased. He often tried to tell his son that it wasn't always the strikers who got the glory.

Spain scored a second goal after half-time, moving a step closer to the Gold Medal Game. René stood up. 'Game over,' he said.

In a flash, Sergio picked up a cushion and threw it in his brother's direction. 'Don't say that!' he shouted. 'You'll jinx us. There's still time for Ghana to come back. We have to stay focused.'

'When did you start managing the team, little bro?' René shot back, laughing. 'You're right, though. If Ghana score now, it'll be a nervy finish.'

'Well, it'll be your fault if they do!' Sergio said, with a look that said he was only half-joking. But

there was no reason to worry. Spain held on for a
2–0 win, setting up an even bigger game against
Poland in the final just three days later.

But that felt like a long wait for Sergio. When
the Gold Medal Game finally arrived, he was too
distracted to eat his breakfast.

'My stomach is doing backflips,' he explained,
lying on the sofa. 'Just give me a minute.'

'Kiko and Luis Enrique are probably nervous too,'
Paqui said. 'But they have to eat, otherwise they'll
have no energy for the match.'

'Good point,' he said, slowly sitting up and joining
the family at the table.

By kick-off, Sergio was already pacing around
the living room. 'Win or lose, we should all be very
proud of the team,' Paqui explained, fearing how
Sergio would react if Spain lost.

But Sergio barely heard her. He was too busy
watching the Spain players walking down the tunnel
and onto the pitch. Their red shirts looked even
cooler today.

Over the next two hours, Sergio went through

every possible emotion. He had his head in his hands
when Poland scored first, then there was relief and
joy as Spain came back to lead 2–1. Then frustration
as Poland made it 2–2 almost immediately. Now,
extra time was looming.

With ninety minutes on the clock, Spain won
a corner. 'Come on, one last chance,' Paqui said,
with her hands over her face. Sergio was silent, just
praying for a late winner.

The ball came in and was cleared to the edge of
the box.

'Shoot!' the family all shouted.

The ball was blocked but it rebounded straight
to Kiko.

'Yes! Yes!' Sergio screamed.

The keeper was already on the floor, having dived
for the first shot. Kiko took a quick touch and calmly
lifted the ball into the net.

'Goooooooooal! We've won it! We've won it!'
Sergio yelled, running to hug everyone.

'Wow!' José María, René and Sergio's sister
Miriam all said at once.

They cheered even louder when they saw the replay of the goal.

The phone rang. It was one of José María's friends. He rushed out of the room and was back within a minute. 'That was Jorge. He's going to drive around Camas to see the celebrations. Do you mind if I go?'

'No problem – go for it,' said Paqui. 'But take the kids. They'll love it!'

Sergio raced to the front door, put on his shoes in record time, and then followed José María, Miriam and René out to the car. They drove around Camas, honking the horn all the way and singing songs with friends and neighbours.

España! España! España!

'What a night!' Sergio shouted, hugging René. In his head, he was imagining himself playing football for Spain one day. 'It must be amazing to give the fans a moment like this!'

CHAPTER 3

PEPITO THE SECRET WEAPON

The Olympics had put Sergio firmly on the football path. That continued as he played more often at the park, often begging René to let him join in with the older kids when they needed an extra player, or tag along for his Camas Juniors practices.

'Please can I play? Pleeeeaaaase – I won't let you down, I promise!'

One morning, he finally got his wish. Paqui hurried down the stairs and packed shorts and socks into René's bag.

'Change of plans,' she called, stopping to catch her breath. 'Sergio, you're coming with us to René's practice and then we'll go straight to the festival.'

Sergio grinned and rushed to the front door quickly before his mum could change her mind. He loved watching his brother play, and he would get to dribble his ball around and take some practice shots on the pitch opposite.

René looked over at his younger brother as they left the house. 'I don't mind you coming to the practice, but just don't say anything embarrassing in front of my friends.'

They weaved their way through the narrow streets of Camas and turned into the car park just in time. Sergio saw the familiar faces of René's teammates on the nearest pitch starting their warm-up.

'Okay, out you get,' Paqui said.

René undid his seat belt and hopped out to join his friends. Paqui turned to Sergio as he followed his brother. 'Sergio, remember, just stay close. I'll be here if you need me.'

Sergio nodded and dribbled over to the touchline to get a closer look at the action. He could see René's coach laying out cones and pointing for the boys to line up on the edge of the penalty area.

As Sergio flicked the ball up and trapped it expertly with his right foot, he felt a hand on his shoulder. He turned to see Nando, one of René's best friends.

'Hey, Sergio,' he said. 'So, is this some kind of punishment? Watching your brother play football can be tough on the eyes.'

Sergio laughed. 'I'll tell him you said that!'

'Please do! Are you getting to play much yet?'

'Just with friends at the park. Hopefully my parents will sign me up for a proper team next season.'

'Cool! Come and take some shots. I'll go in goal.'

Sergio paused. 'Wait, why aren't you training with the others?'

'I hurt my knee last week and they want me to rest it. Don't worry – I won't be diving around.'

'Okay, you're on!'

Sergio suddenly felt a bit nervous as he walked over. He knew Nando was a good player and he didn't want to make a fool of himself.

He lined up the ball near the penalty spot, took a few steps backwards and kicked it as hard as he could. His shot went straight at Nando, who saved it easily, but Sergio was pleased with the power.

'Nice one!' Nando called out. 'Just angle your foot a bit to aim it into the corner.'

Sergio had another try, going for the same power but better direction. He looked up to see the ball sweeping into the bottom corner.

Goooooooooooooooooooaaaaaaaaaaaaaaaaaallllllllllll llllllllllllllll!!!!!!!!!!!!!!!!!!!!

He tried to hide his excitement, but a smile quickly spread across his face.

'Perfect!' Nando shouted as he picked the ball out of the net. 'You'll be teaching your brother how to play in no time!'

Sergio felt ten feet tall. Now he had the confidence to run back to the halfway line and dribble forward for his next shot – a little touch with his right foot, right foot again, then left, then right. As he got into the penalty area, he took one quick look at the goal and poked the ball into the net.

Goooooooooooooooooooaaaaaaaaaaaaaaaaaallllllllllll llllllllllllllll!!!!!!!!!!!!!!!!!!!!

28

Sergio had forgotten all about René's practice. He loved that he had the chance to test himself.

After a few more shots, Nando walked over and patted Sergio on the back. 'You've got a lot better since I last saw you. Keep it up.' He handed the ball back to Sergio. 'I better go before I get in trouble with the coaches.'

Sergio went back over to watch his brother.

By now, they had split into teams of three to play matches on small pitches. He could hear one of the coaches shouting instructions, reminding the boys to focus on one-touch passes.

As he waited for the practice to finish, he dribbled up and down the touchline – first at a slow, careful pace and then faster and faster. He was sweating now and stopped near the corner flag to catch his breath.

He looked up to see one of the coaches walking over. His heart sank. Was the coach angry that Nando had been risking his knee injury to play with him? His mind spun round quickly as he tried to think of what he would say.

But as the coach got closer, Sergio could see that he was smiling. Maybe this was about something else.

'You're René's brother, right?'

Sergio nodded.

'I'm Hector, one of the main coaches working with Camas Juniors. Do you want to join in with us? We could use another player to even up the teams.'

Sergio's mouth dropped open. 'Yes, sure,' he finally managed to reply, then immediately wondered what René would say.

He followed Hector over to the pitch and retied his shoelaces.

Lolo, the other coach, was now sorting the boys into two teams to play on a bigger pitch. 'Lolo, we've got one more here,' Hector called, pointing to Sergio.

René laughed, putting an arm round Sergio. 'I should have known there was no chance of you just kicking the ball around quietly!'

Once the game started, Sergio loved every minute of it. He couldn't kick the ball as hard or as far as the other boys, but he raced around the pitch and made a couple of clearances.

Then the ball deflected towards him. He controlled it well, looked up and poked a quick pass to René, who drilled a low shot into the bottom corner.

'Great pass, little bro!' René said, putting Sergio in a playful headlock.

As the boys scooped up their water bottles at the end of the practice, Lolo joined René and Sergio.

'Well done today – both of you. Sergio, you've got great instincts and you don't even seem tired after all that running. Are you already signed up for a team this year?'

Sergio shook his head, and a little smile appeared in the corner of Lolo's mouth.

'How would you like to sign with Camas Juniors?'
Sergio was stunned and confused.

René had the same look of shock on his face. 'I like playing with Sergio, especially when he gives me passes like that one today, but he's only seven. Isn't our league really strict on checking ages? If he's not nine yet, how can he play?'

But Sergio could see from Lolo's face that he had a plan. 'Well, we might be in luck here. We've got a completed registration form for a boy called Pepito, but his dad had to change jobs, so they've moved to another town. I'm thinking you could play as Pepito. What do you think?'

At first, Sergio and René both laughed, but then they realised that Lolo was serious. 'Really?' Sergio asked.

'I don't usually like to bend the rules, but a player with your energy would really help us and the season is only a few weeks away.'

'Wow, okay. I'll have to ask my mum and dad, but I'm sure they'll let me play. They've got to drive René to games anyway.'

René nodded. 'Welcome to the team, Pepito!'

They all burst out laughing.

CHAPTER 4

DREAMING BIG

Señor Nunez waved his hands and whistled to get his class's attention. 'This morning, we're going to get into groups to talk about the types of jobs you might like to do when you're older. That might seem like a long way away – and it is – but it's a good exercise to get you thinking.'

He took a piece of chalk and started writing on the board, giving the class some examples to consider.

'Some of you might like to teach, like me.' He paused and grinned at the silence in the room. 'I guess not! Maybe a doctor or a racing car driver is more exciting. See what you can come up with.'

He split the class into five groups and then

walked around the room listening to the different conversations.

'I used to think I wanted to be a matador and put on a show for a big crowd,' Sergio explained to his group, as Señor Nunez appeared and sat on the edge of the desk. 'But now that I've started playing football every week, I've changed my mind. I'm going to be a professional footballer in La Liga!'

His teacher looked at him with a raised eyebrow. 'Sergio, having a dream to chase is never a bad thing, but you also have to remember that only the very best can play football as their job. It's important to have other options too.'

'But football is all I want to do,' Sergio insisted. 'I love it. If I work hard enough, I know I can do it.'

Señor Nunez nodded. 'Well, you've certainly got the right attitude. Just keep an open mind about a Plan B.'

He didn't want to upset Sergio, but he felt a responsibility to be honest about the difficult odds of becoming a footballer. He had seen it before – so many good young players were fighting to get into the big academies and there were no guarantees. But Sergio was clearly talented. Señor Nunez had heard the stories about lunchtime hat-tricks and weekend victories. Maybe he could beat the odds, after all.

When Sergio got home from school, he went straight to the back garden and started knocking a ball back and forth against the wall, testing his reactions as it pinged back towards him. Then he switched to keepy-ups. He was determined to prove his teacher wrong.

Hearing the sound, Paqui looked out of the kitchen window. She knew the signs with Sergio. Something had made him angry.

'What's wrong, Sergio?' she called. When he didn't reply, she walked outside and asked him again.

Sergio picked up the ball. Sweat was pouring down his face. 'Nothing really. Señor Nunez told me that it's really hard to become a professional footballer, but I'm going to show him I can be that one out of thousands who makes it.'

Paqui smiled. She had learned long ago not to

make the kind of mistake that Sergio's teacher had made. When her son set his heart on achieving something, he was an unstoppable force.

'Just be careful, darling,' she pleaded. 'You're already playing against older kids at the weekend. I don't want you to be too tired or fall behind at school.'

'I've got it covered,' Sergio replied with a wink. 'You worry too much, Mum!'

The back garden practices became a regular event as he tried to improve his ball control, passing and shooting. Sometimes René joined in, and José María too. Sergio put sticks in the ground to dribble in and out of when he was by himself, and two tall, skinny trees were the perfect goalposts. Often, he was out there until the last sliver of sunlight had gone.

René was still bigger and stronger than his younger brother, but Sergio made up for it with his energy and fearlessness. Plus, he was getting more and more skilful. One night, just after Paqui had given them the five-minute warning for dinner, Sergio wrong-footed René with a quick change of direction and smashed a low shot into the imaginary bottom corner, glancing off the inside of the tree trunk.

José María and René exchanged a quick glance that silently said: 'Wow, Sergio is getting really good!'

Sergio pretended not to see it, but he could hardly contain a grin as he jogged back down the garden.

CHAPTER 5

SCOUTED BY SEVILLA

Sergio started off as a secret with Camas Juniors, but it did not stay that way for long. The more he played, the faster his game developed, and he was soon one of the first names on the team sheet.

Then one Saturday, when he was ten years old, his world was turned upside down. For weeks, he had heard stories from friends about scouts coming to watch local games. Each time, he had laughed at the idea, but deep down that extra pressure made him nervous. What if he made a bad mistake? Would the scouts know that he was younger than the rest of the boys?

'Try not to think about that,' José María said,

sensing that Sergio was getting distracted. 'It's just another game. Go out and enjoy yourself.'

Lolo had a similar message for the team. 'Don't try to be the hero and do too much on your own. Play as a team – the way we always do.'

Sergio felt sharp. It was usually at the end of games that his energy stood out, as other boys got tired. But today he felt a step quicker than everyone else, right from the first whistle.

One minute he was sprinting towards a loose ball and playing a quick pass down the line, the next he was winning two tackles to stop a counter-attack. Sergio knew he was rarely the most skilful player on the pitch, but he made up for it with his speed and his brain.

At half-time, José María put an arm round Sergio. 'Awesome!' he said quietly. 'That's the best half I've ever seen you play.'

At the end of the game, Sergio was exhausted. He limped over with his teammates and sat down on the grass, breathing heavily. Usually his dad came over with Sergio's water bottle and some words of encouragement – but not today. He spotted José María on the opposite side of the pitch and saw his dad talking with a tall man in a tracksuit. Sergio had never seen him before.

'Well done today,' Lolo was explaining, but Sergio was only half-listening. Who was this mystery man talking to his dad?

Finally, his dad appeared and weaved his way through the tired boys gathered around their coach. He ruffled Sergio's hair and passed him his water. Sergio turned to thank him and saw a huge smile on his dad's face. José María winked and then walked away, not wanting to interrupt the coach's post-game talk.

When it was time to go, Sergio rushed over to his dad, ready to ask a hundred questions. José María had been planning to keep it a secret until they were back in the car, but when he saw the excited look on his son's face, the words just tumbled out.

'You're not going to believe this, Sergio,' he began. 'A scout from Sevilla was at the game today and you really impressed him! He wants you to come for some training sessions at their academy. The director is going to phone tonight with more details.'

Sergio's legs turned to jelly. 'Wow!' was all he managed to say. He had hoped that the mystery man might be a scout, but he hadn't dared to dream.

That night, José María, Paqui and Sergio waited patiently for the call from Sevilla. Just before nine o'clock, the phone rang, and his dad hurried to the kitchen to answer it.

'Hello, José María speaking.'

'Hi there – sorry to call so late. This is Pablo Blanco, director of the Sevilla academy. I got a glowing report from one of my scouts today about Sergio – he's clearly a natural. You must be very proud.'

'Thank you – we are. Sergio just loves to play football.'

'Well, there's obviously potential there. We'd like to offer Sergio an eight-week trial at the academy, starting on Wednesday. Training starts at seven o'clock, but can you come in a little earlier to sign the paperwork? Then we'll introduce Sergio to the coaches.'

As Pablo was talking, José María took a second to give Sergio a thumbs-up. 'That's fantastic,' he replied. 'Yes, we'll be there!' René and Miriam had heard the phone ring and appeared in the doorway.

When José María put the phone down, he turned to the rest of his family.

'Wrong number, I guess,' he said, laughing.

'Yeah, right,' Sergio replied, grinning. 'Come on, what did they say?'

'Do you have any plans on Wednesday night? If not, you'll be training with the Sevilla academy. They're giving you a trial!'

'Woooooooooooooo!' Sergio, René and Miriam shouted all at once. They came together with their parents for a big family hug.

'Congratulations, little bro,' René said. 'This could be the start of something really special. Just remember that I'm the one who taught you everything you know!'

'I've got to call my friends and tell them the

news,' Sergio said suddenly. 'What a day! They won't believe it!'

But José María was already holding up one hand to put an end to that plan. 'It's late, Sergio. They'll be in bed. That's where you need to be too.'

He expected big protests from Sergio about how he would never be able to sleep with all the excitement, but his son just nodded. 'You're right. I can't be tired on Wednesday.' He disappeared and came back in his pyjamas to say goodnight.

The next three days were painfully slow for Sergio. One minute, he was nervous about whether he would be good enough to compete against boys who had probably been at the academy for a few years already. The next minute, it was pure excitement. His friends talked about it non-stop, and asked a barrage of questions. Would he meet the players? Would he be practising at the stadium? What would he be doing in the sessions?

Sergio had none of the answers, though. 'You'll have to wait for Thursday morning,' he said. 'No bad tackles in the playground until then, please.'

On the Wednesday afternoon, both Sergio and his father hurried home.

'We can't be late, Sergio,' José María called. 'There's some chicken and rice in the fridge. Start eating that and then get changed.'

The car journey to meet with Pablo was mostly a quiet one. Sergio looked out of the window and thought about what he would say when he met the other boys.

'You're going to be great,' his dad said, mainly to break the silence and help Sergio relax. 'But the most important thing is to have fun. If you do that, good things will happen.'

A smiling man met them at reception and then Pablo appeared from one of the hallways. 'José María – nice to meet you! And this must be Sergio. Welcome to the Sevilla academy. Follow me.'

They made their way to a big office with windows that looked out onto the pitches below.

'Okay, we'll get to the forms and signatures in a minute. That part is easy. But first, Sergio, I want you to know that we're very excited to have you here with us at Sevilla. I'm sure you'll get on very well with the other boys and all the coaches.'

There was a knock on the door. 'Ah, perfect timing. José María, we can finish the paperwork together. Sergio, there are some people I want you to meet. Come in!'

A man in a tracksuit with a friendly face walked in.

'This is Agustín, who will be coaching you tonight,' Pablo explained. 'He runs the Under 10s team.'

Sergio stood up and shook hands. He wasn't sure how much to say, so he settled on 'I can't wait to get started.'

Two boys appeared behind Agustín, who promptly introduced them. 'Sergio, this is Antonio and this is Javier. We wanted there to be a few familiar faces by the time you get out onto the pitch.'

Sergio shook hands again.

'Boys, can you show Sergio around? There's a training top for him in the changing room. I'll see you out on the pitch in twenty minutes.'

Sergio said bye to Agustín, Pablo and his dad, then followed Antonio and Javier.

'The coaches make everything really fun,' Antonio said. 'I'm sure you'll enjoy it.'

'I remember being pretty nervous at my first training session, but it went away as soon as they got the balls out and we started playing,' Javier added, and then he came to a stop. 'Here we are – this is where we get ready.'

Javier was right. It didn't take long for Sergio to shake off the nerves. During the warm-up, he hit a couple of crisp passes and managed to match the others' pace on their laps of the pitch. From then on, he felt at home.

Even so, Sergio still needed to give the Sevilla youth coaches a reason to keep him around. When they switched to five-a-side games, Sergio sensed his chance to shine. He was everywhere, sprinting back to make important tackles, playing the simple pass and even scoring a couple of goals. When Agustín called for a water break, Sergio bent over, panting, and tried to catch his breath. His legs ached, he had a cut on his knee that was bleeding, and his shirt was soaked with sweat. But he was loving it.

At the end of the practice, Agustín gathered the boys together. 'Great session today,' he said. 'You moved the ball well and we were sharp around the box. Sergio, you looked right at home with us too. Great job.'

Sergio felt a shiver of excitement and tried to play it cool as some of the other boys looked over at him. Even after showering and changing, he still had a big smile on his face. When he saw his dad waiting for him outside, he noticed that he was grinning too.

'So, how was the first practice?' José María asked.

'Amazing!' Sergio said. 'At first, I was nervous, but I was just as good as the other boys, and you should have seen one of my sliding tackles!'

José María laughed. 'Only you would dish out some bruises in your first academy session!'

'I can't wait for the next practice! I just hope I can do enough to make them keep me for longer.'

'It's funny you should say that,' José María

replied. 'Agustín came to see me while you were getting changed. He's already talking about signing you!'

Sergio's mouth dropped open, but no words came out. He just smiled all the way home.

CHAPTER 6

ANTONIO AND JESÚS

Sergio was one of the fastest rising stars in the
Sevilla academy, but his progress was not without
challenges. For a start, he could play in a few
different positions and that meant he got moved all
over the pitch. He also spent some time watching
from the touchline after injuring his leg. But through
it all, he had first Antonio Puerta, then Jesús Navas
too, to turn to. Whatever the situation, the 'three
amigos', as they liked to call themselves, were there
for each other.

Antonio liked to think of himself as the wise old
man. He had been at the Sevilla academy the longest
and knew everyone around the place, from the

cafeteria ladies to the cleaners. He and Sergio moved through the Under-11s, Under-12s and Under-13s together, sweeping aside every team they faced. With Sergio now fit again after missing their Under-14 season, he was ready to face the best Under-15 teams in the country – and now they had Jesús, the new kid on the block, on the team too. Antonio and Sergio liked him from the very first practice.

Sergio was spending more and more time at the academy, training a few times a week, and then coming in to put in extra work between sessions. More often than not, at least one of the other amigos was with him.

Their friendships made a big difference on the pitch. Since all three were playing in midfield, they knew exactly where each other would be at all times. Whether it was a perfect through ball or a pinpoint cross, they had an unspoken understanding of how to play football.

During one away game, Sevilla were losing 1–0, before the three amigos turned it around. 'We're not losing this,' Sergio said to Antonio and Jesús as the second half began. First, Sergio beat two defenders and squared the ball to Jesús for a tap-in. Then Antonio skipped through, rounded the keeper and was tripped up. Before the referee could blow the whistle for a penalty, Sergio had pounced on the loose ball and fired it into the net.

'The three of us are unstoppable,' Antonio said as they sat outside at the Ramos house eating ice cream. He had become a regular visitor there and both Paqui and José María thought he was a great influence on Sergio. He went on: 'Sometimes I think about what it would be like if we all got into the first team together.'

'We'd have so much fun,' Sergio added. 'The coaches would never be able to get us to stop talking, but they'd still love us!'

'Plus, we'd get to hang out even more. That means more card games, more films, more parties.'

'Life doesn't get much better than that,' Jesús said.

They all laughed. They were living the dream.

'Most of all, it's pretty cool to get to play the game you love with great friends,' Sergio said. 'The academy would be a lonely place in some ways if we hadn't met.'

Their run of wins continued – one week 4–0, the next week 5–1. At school, word spread about their success with Sevilla, but all that attention didn't change them. René was always the first to bring Sergio back down to earth if he got too cocky. 'It's for your own good, little bro,' he liked to say, wagging his finger. 'You'll thank me one day!'

But that kind of advice was rarely needed. The three amigos were usually too busy talking about the last game, thinking about the next one and planning their eventual domination of La Liga as Sevilla's biggest stars.

CHAPTER 7

ON THE FAST TRACK TO THE TOP!

Sergio pinged the ball across to Jesús, who controlled it on his chest and passed it back.

'I'm telling you, Jesús, we're going to win the Under-16 League and the Cup this year,' Sergio said. 'I've got a good feeling about it.'

Jesús grinned. 'You always say that about everything! Seriously, when was the last time you had a bad feeling about anything?! But this time you might be right.'

'We're going to surprise people. With you on one wing, Antonio on the other and me at the back, we can beat anyone.'

Sergio was playing more and more in defence,

using his speed to cut out through balls and his passing to start attacks. He had grown too and was winning lots of headers.

Toni, one of the newer coaches, called the players together and they set off on a few laps around the pitch.

At the end of training, Sergio felt a tap on his shoulder. 'Just hold on a minute,' Toni said, looking around to check whether the other players had all started walking back inside. 'Another good session today. Well done.'

'Thanks, Coach.'

'You'll thank me even more when you hear this.'

Sergio looked up, confused but excited.

'I got a call this morning from Joaquín Caparrós. He's been keeping a close eye on you.'

The first team boss! Sergio grinned. He had seen the first team coaches at practices and games occasionally, but they had usually gone by the time the sessions finished.

'I'll get right to the point. Caparrós wants you to start training with the first team.'

Sergio tried to look calm but inside he was jumping up and down. He was going to be sharing the same pitch with the players he watched on TV every weekend.

When he got dropped off at home, Sergio raced up the street and bundled through the door. 'Mum! Dad!'

His parents rushed out of the kitchen, with panic on their faces. 'What's wrong?' Paqui asked.

'Nothing – sorry, I didn't mean to scare you. I just have big news and I couldn't wait to tell you.'

'What? Tell us!'

'I'm going to be training with the first team!'

They rushed over and wrapped Sergio in a big hug.

'My son is going to be training with the Sevilla first team!' José María kept saying over and over.

Once Sergio had finished telling all his friends and family, the excitement was at least partly replaced by nerves. What if it was a big disaster? He was only sixteen and now he would be playing against men.

Just then, his phone rang. It was Jesús.

'Congrats, mate. I just saw your text.'

'What if I blow this chance, Jesús? I've worked so hard over the last few years. We all have.'

'You won't. I know you and so do the coaches.

They wouldn't have called you up if they didn't think you were ready to take this next step. I bet they'll all give you a warm welcome. If you play like you always do in our practices, you'll be fine.'

'Thanks. I've just got a lot on my mind and this is all happening really fast.'

'That's what I'm here for. We'll miss you, though. I guess that's the end of our plan to win the league and cup together.'

'No,' Sergio replied instantly. 'It means that we're going to do it together in the first team. Just wait and see.'

The next day, he got dropped off at the training ground extra early. He couldn't risk being late on his first morning with the first team.

Caparrós spotted him roaming the corridors and called him over.

'Couldn't sleep?' he asked, smiling.

Sergio blushed. 'Something like that,' he replied.

'This is a big moment for me.'

'It is,' Caparrós agreed. 'But try not to over-think it. We believe in you and you're going to get plenty of chances to learn. The lads are excited to meet you.'

Caparrós introduced him to a few of the players, and then – once they were out on the pitch – gave him a proper welcome in front of the whole squad.

The first session went well. His control was good, and he felt confident enough to use both feet, even though he was always more comfortable on his right foot. If anything, he got a bit *too* confident. During one of the exercises, he was one of the two 'piggies in the middle', closing down other players as they tried to knock the ball around the circle. As he sprinted around, he spotted a pass that was hit a little too softly. In a flash, he lunged forward and poked the ball away, but at the same time he collided with one of his teammates.

Sergio turned to see that he had injured Pablo Alfaro, the Sevilla captain and one of the toughest, most feared defenders in La Liga. His heart skipped a beat – this was the last person he wanted as an enemy. He walked over slowly and put his hand on Pablo's back. 'Sorry. I didn't see you.'

Pablo gave him a long stare, and then broke out into a little grin. 'No worries, kid. That was a tackle I'd be proud of.'

Sergio was thrilled to be learning so much from his older teammates – and his coaches seemed to be really pleased with his progress. One January afternoon, Caparrós walked over to the pitch with Sergio and, without any big build up, said:

'You'll be on the bench on Wednesday night against Deportivo. We're really impressed with the way you've trained over the past few weeks and now it's time to start getting you some playing time.'

'This isn't a joke, is it?' Sergio answered, laughing.

He was still only seventeen years old. 'Don't do that to me!'

Caparrós smiled. 'That would be so cruel! No, I'm serious.'

As he climbed the steps onto the team bus for the

drive to the airport, Sergio had butterflies. He was travelling with all the same players that he trained with every day, but somehow this felt different. He was making his La Liga debut!

With Sevilla losing 1–0 to Deportivo, Sergio started warming up again, stretching and jogging up and down the touchline. On his way back to the dugout, Caparrós signalled for him to come over.

'We're sending you on in five minutes for Francisco so stay ready.'

'Will do, boss.' Sergio hoped his voice didn't sound too nervous. His heart was racing.

He finished a few more stretches and started taking off his tracksuit. He wondered if his friends and family at home could see him. He was sure there would be a lot of calls and texts flying around.

The ball was cleared out for a throw-in and the referee stopped play for the substitution. Sergio was coming on! He jumped up and down a couple of times, high-fived Francisco and then ran on to join his teammates.

With less than thirty minutes of the game left,

Sergio – playing at right-back – was determined
to make an impact. When the ball went out for a
throw-in on the far side, he allowed himself a couple
of seconds to look around the pitch and savour the
moment. This was really happening!

*

That summer, as he sat outside and enjoyed a family
barbeque, Sergio was glad of the rest. It had been a
whirlwind year.

'If I'd told you a year ago that you would soon
be making your debut for the first team, would you
have believed me?' René asked.

'No chance,' Sergio replied, laughing. 'I'd have
thought you were crazy. But the coaches have faith
in me, and I think next season could be a really big
one for me.'

No matter what he did, he couldn't take his mind
off football. Even a short holiday didn't do the trick.
All he wanted was to be in the gym and out on the
pitch working on his game.

When pre-season finally rolled round, Sergio

immediately stood out as being one of the best.

'He looks stronger, fitter and more confident,' one of the assistants pointed out.

The others agreed. 'Sergio has done everything we've asked. I think it's time to throw him into the deep end and start him at right-back this season.'

CHAPTER 8

BERNABÉU BOUND

Sergio's first full season in La Liga flew by, with the club finishing sixth. He surprised himself with how quickly he adapted to life as a pro – and people were taking notice. One morning as he walked out to his car after training, his phone rang. It was Luis Aragonés, the Spanish national team manager, or '*El Sabio*' ('The Wise Man') as most people called him.

For a split second, Sergio thought it might be a prank from one of his teammates, but he recognised the manager's voice.

'I'll keep it short, Sergio,' he said. 'We've picked you in the squad for the friendly against China next month. You've had a terrific season and we believe you'll be playing for Spain for many years to come.'

Sergio was speechless for a moment. 'Wow, that's amazing news,' he said. 'Thank you. I won't let you down.'

He didn't even have time to call all his family and friends before the news broke. On his drive home, his phone pinged again and again with new text messages.

Sergio's mum burst into tears as soon as he called his parents to tell them the news, while he could feel his dad's pride through the phone. 'It feels like only yesterday that we were watching the '92 Olympics together and imagining what it would be like if one of our children was part of it,' he said.

When Sergio joined up with the squad in Salamanca, he was as nervous as he could ever remember being. He was training with the some of the same players he had grown up idolising, and he was thankful that he got a warm welcome from them all.

On game day, he walked into the dressing room

before the warm-up and froze on the spot. The famous red shirts were hanging all around the dressing room and in the back corner, he saw his name on one of them: RAMOS. He had always loved playing for his country at youth levels – and that pride was multiplied by a hundred for the senior team. He took a photo on his phone and sent it to all his family with a simple caption: 'Blessed'.

After a national anthem that made his whole body tingle, he jogged over to his position at right-back and did a few final stretches. 'This is so crazy,' he thought to himself. He had a few loose touches early on, but the jitters soon passed, and he played his part in a 3–0 win. Before they left the dressing room, his teammates all signed his shirt, which made it a prized souvenir for the rest of his life.

*

Back at Sevilla, the fans had fallen in love with Sergio – his physical style, his tough tackling and his bold forward runs. Many already saw him as a future club captain. But the mighty Real Madrid had other ideas.

They were tracking him closely as they tried to turn their fortunes around ahead of the 2005/06 season, and that meant some difficult conversations for the club's President, Florentino Pérez.

'We've got to do something about our defence,' one senior Real Madrid advisor explained. 'Even with all our Galácticos, we can't win every game 5–4.'

The room went quiet. Signing defenders was always a touchy subject.

'Look, I know it's not the flashy approach we're known for, but it's the only way forward,' the advisor continued, hoping to see nods around the table.

'But we've talked for months about signing a striker,' Pérez replied. 'Attacking football is what people think of with Real Madrid and we have a long history to protect.'

The conversation eventually shifted to which defenders might be available, and there was discussion about the pros and cons of each.

'Sergio Ramos at Sevilla is an interesting option

too,' Pérez said suddenly. 'He's only nineteen, but the boy can play. He loves to get forward too.'

There were nods as he said this and then everyone tried to talk at once.

'But he's still a bit raw and a bit reckless,' said one voice. 'Don't we want someone who can contribute for us straight away?'

'If we're going to buy a defender, that's the kind of guy we want,' argued another. 'He's a winner.'

'Okay then,' Pérez interrupted. 'We'll check on him and see what it would take to bring him here.'

'He's got a buyout clause with Sevilla,' a director explained. 'That should help us.'

Sergio had been in the league long enough to know that rumours could appear out of the blue, with no facts behind them. But he still gasped when he saw the report that Real Madrid were interested in signing him.

He called René, who had taken over as his agent and manager. 'I just saw the update. Real Madrid? Really? What's going on?'

'I was just about to call you. I'm trying to find

out if there's any truth to it, just to be prepared. The ball would be in Sevilla's court though. You're still under contract.'

'Okay, cool. Keep me posted.'

Sergio tried not to think about it. After all, he loved life at Sevilla, and everyone had been so supportive... but this was Real Madrid. Or at least it *might* be Real Madrid. He found himself daydreaming about playing in that famous white shirt at the Bernabéu.

When René called back later that day, he confirmed that conversations were underway between the two clubs. 'Your release clause is €27 million. We just have to wait and see whether Real Madrid are willing to pay it.'

Sergio could hardly believe it. That would make him the most expensive Spanish defender... *ever!*

With his head still spinning, Sergio hoped that things would be decided quickly, one way or the other. Sevilla president José María del Nido knew that Sergio was the type of young talent that would fit in at any big club and make an impact. He was

determined to demand a fair price that could help
the Sevilla team rebuild itself.

'There's not much we can do to push this
forward,' René explained as the negotiations rolled
on. 'Just be patient. My gut tells me a deal will
eventually happen.'

In the meantime, Sergio was trapped. He saw
his face on every sports show and every newspaper.
The gym was one of the few places where he
could find some peace and quiet, but the idea of
letting down the Sevilla fans caused his stomach to
constantly ache.

Finally, he got the call from René. 'Sergio, we're
still sorting a few final things, but the deal is going
through. Just wanted you to know. I can say it out
loud now – my brother is going to be playing for
Real Madrid!'

Sergio felt a strange mix of happiness, relief and
sadness. This was an incredible opportunity to make
his mark at one of the world's biggest clubs, but
it was Sevilla who had given him his chance as a
professional.

After the meetings, René went straight to see Sergio.

'Little bro,' said René, 'do you realise that you are the only Spanish player that Florentino Pérez has signed in the past few years? Real Madrid really fought for you.'

Sergio half-smiled and nodded.

'What's wrong?' René asked. 'I thought we'd be celebrating tonight.'

'I'm excited,' Sergio said. 'I really am. But it's tough to turn my back on Sevilla.'

René nodded. 'I get it. But think of it this way, they got a huge transfer fee for you. That sets Sevilla up for years to come – all because of you.'

'Hmmm, I hadn't thought of it like that,' Sergio replied.

'And what reasonable fan could really blame you for being happy about signing for Real Madrid?'

Sergio laughed. 'I bet there are a few. Even some of my friends, I guess. But you're right. This is a special moment and I'm ruining it by being moody. Let's go see Mum and Dad and celebrate the news together.'

Pérez called Sergio an hour later. 'Welcome to Real Madrid, Sergio!' he said. 'We can't wait to see you at the Bernabéu for the press conference. For now, I wanted to ask if you were happy with the Number 4 shirt. It has a special place in our history and Fernando Hierro has just retired. We think you're the kind of player who can follow in those footsteps.'

'This all still feels like a dream if I'm being completely honest,' Sergio said. 'But, yes, Number 4 sounds great.'

'Great, we'll have that ready for the press conference.'

They went through all the arrangements for travelling to Madrid for Sergio's medical. He did his best to follow the conversation, but a thousand thoughts were flying through his head. He grabbed a sheet of paper and scribbled some notes so he would remember the key points.

Sergio had seen the videos of other players joining Real Madrid, but those were superstars like Zinedine Zidane and David Beckham. He did not expect many people to show up for his introduction, but he was stunned to see huge crowds to welcome him.

'Sergio! Sergio! We love you!'

'You're the man to put us back on top!'

The day flew by, with questions, camera flashes and lots of smiling. When he finally got back to his hotel, he turned on the TV but fell asleep on the sofa before he could even choose a film to watch.

'There's so much still to do,' he told Miriam the next morning as he packed up to come home. 'But the club has booked the same hotel for me for the first few months so I can slowly start looking for a place to live.'

'We're here to help too. I can come up for a weekend and help you settle in.'

José María and Paqui couldn't let Sergio leave without a big party. They called cousins, aunts, uncles, friends and neighbours, and the back garden was full of familiar faces when Sergio arrived. 'You told me it was just a few friends!' he said to his mum, laughing. 'At least I know I've got a few fans here even I'm a flop at Real Madrid!'

CHAPTER 9

GETTING ON WITH THE GALÁCTICOS

When the first day of Real Madrid's pre-season training arrived, Sergio felt a different energy – the car park had been deserted when he dropped in for his medical; now there were fancy cars everywhere. The Galácticos were in the building!

Sergio vaguely remembered his way around and found the dressing room without too many wrong turns. He tried not to stare as he walked in, keeping his head down and finding his training kit neatly lined up at his locker. But once he sat down it was impossible not to watch what was going on around him.

To his left, Beckham and Zidane were looking at new Adidas boots that had just been delivered for them to try out. To his right, Roberto Carlos and Ronaldo were swapping stories with Robinho, another summer signing. Opposite him, Raúl, Iker Casillas and Michel Salgado were planning a pre-season party.

Somehow, Sergio was now part of this scene. At least he already knew some of the Spanish players.

Iker spotted him and guessed that he might be a little nervous. Rather than shouting across the dressing room and putting all eyes on Sergio, he just walked over and gave him a big hug.

'Hey Sergio, welcome to Real Madrid. It's great to see you – I've been waiting for the club to put some decent defenders in front of me!'

Michel came over to give Iker a playful jab in the ribs. 'I heard that!' He shook hands with Sergio. 'Come and meet the rest of the lads.'

'We needed another Spaniard around here,' Raúl said with a big grin. 'We can't have the Brazilians running the place.'

Everyone laughed, especially Ronaldo and Roberto Carlos, who both came over and put an arm on Sergio's shoulder.

'You'll love it here,' said Ronaldo.

Sergio smiled and remembered his mum's words as he left the house to travel to Madrid. 'Don't be shy. I'm sure they're all just regular guys away from the cameras.' She was right.

Later that week, his family arrived in Madrid to spend a few days with him. All they wanted to know about was life with the Galácticos. Luckily, he had no shortage of stories. Being around some of the greatest players ever was never dull, and the flicks and tricks he saw in training were unlike anything he could even dream of trying.

'Remember how we used to make fantasy football teams with all the best players?' René said. 'Now you're playing on one of those teams!'

But after feeling starstruck for the first two training sessions, Sergio knew that he would never play his best football if he was constantly thinking of his teammates as superstars and heroes. Instead, he had to think of them as equals. After all, Real Madrid had paid €27 million to sign him; didn't that make him a Galáctico too? Okay, so Sergio didn't score goals like Ronaldo or bend the ball like Beckham, but he was unbeatable at the back. He was the future of the Real defence and it was time to show it.

'Get stuck in,' manager Vanderlei Luxemburgo told him one morning. 'The Galácticos may not always like it, but they'll respect it.'

'Sergio, remember, if you can keep Ronaldo and Raúl quiet in training, the rest of La Liga will feel like a walk in the park,' Iker added.

Once he brought that mindset, life was easier. He was calmer in the passing drills and less afraid to mark them in attack vs defence sessions. By the time the season kicked off, Sergio felt at home. He would probably never be a Galáctico, but he was certainly ready to wear the famous Real Madrid shirt.

But the first few months were a struggle. After one particular low point, Sergio stomped back to the dressing room and sat with his hands over his face. He was furious – partly with the referee but mostly with himself. He had just picked up his third red card of the season and it was only late November.

His first season with Real Madrid was in danger of becoming a nightmare.

How did this keep happening? Today it had been a split-second mistake: he lunged in when he felt confident that he could get the ball. It was a silly decision, especially as he already had a yellow card. When would he learn?

'Chin up, pal,' one of the assistant coaches told Sergio after jogging back to check on him. 'You were unlucky on that one but sometimes you've got to stay on your feet. Think about how Paolo Maldini and Fabio Cannavaro defend.'

Sergio nodded, still staring at the ground. 'It's just been a tough season with all the pressure. I'm a better player than I've shown so far.'

'Don't worry about that,' said the assistant coach. 'Everyone loves you and knows how talented you are. Don't be too hard on yourself. You're still only nineteen.'

Even with all the Galácticos, Real Madrid had a hard time gelling. Having played at right-back for Sevilla, Sergio was sometimes asked to play at centre-back and that was a whole new learning curve.

The 2005/06 season ended in disappointment for Real Madrid and there were plenty of questions from impatient voices inside and outside the club. Sergio had been thrown into a tough situation but, despite some wobbles, he was still standing. That counted as a victory.

'I think Real Madrid knew that my first year would be a bit of a roller coaster,' Sergio told his family after the final game of the season. 'But they've shown faith in me and now I have to prove them right.'

While a few of his teammates prepared for a long summer holiday, Sergio had other plans. A call from El Sabio confirmed that he had been chosen for the Spanish squad for the 2006 World Cup, and would be on the plane to Germany.

'Now I know this is going to be the year that Spain finally win again!' Paqui said proudly when she heard the news. 'Congratulations, darling. I feel better about our chances if *you're* in the squad.'

Sergio laughed. 'You're a bit biased, Mum, but I hope you're right!'

CHAPTER 10

SPAIN'S 'SPECIAL SOMETHING'

From Spain's first practice session when they arrived at their World Cup camp in Germany, El Sabio gave strong hints that Sergio would be starting at right-back, with Carles Puyol and Pablo Ibáñez in the centre. When they lined up for a practice match, Sergio was put with Xavi, Andrés, Iker and the rest of the usual starters.

'I don't want to jinx it, but I think I'm going to be starting,' Sergio whispered down the phone from his hotel room. He had to tell his parents, but didn't want anyone to overhear.

The reply from the phone echoed louder than his whisper. 'Wooooooooooooooooooooo!'

Sergio laughed. 'It's hard to believe, really. I only made my debut for the senior team a year ago. Now I'm at the World Cup!'

'Sergio, you keep thinking that this season was a disappointment, but you had some great games,' José María explained. 'You belong on the big stage and I know you'll prove that over the next few weeks.'

Sergio felt butterflies in his stomach as he thought about all the people back home who would be glued to their TV screens, cheering him on – his family, his school friends, maybe even his old teacher, Señor Nunez. But at the same time, this whole adventure with Spain had been such a whirlwind that he didn't have time to get too nervous. He believed in himself and he was ready to just let things unfold.

Before the kick-off of Spain's opening game, against Ukraine, Sergio went through his usual pre-match routine: the same food, taping his left ankle then his right, pulling on a sweatband for each wrist, and so on. As he walked down the tunnel and out into the electric atmosphere of a packed stadium, he still felt calm.

'Treat it as just another game,' he thought to himself.

It helped, of course, that he had already made his debut for Real Madrid at the noisy Bernabéu and experienced the El Clásico match against Barcelona. No match could ever be more intense than that.

After Spain and Ukraine's national anthems had played, Sergio passed the ball around with Carles Puyol and Xavi. Then he spotted El Sabio on the touchline waving for him to come over.

'Just play your natural, fearless game,' his manager told him. 'I've been around football long enough to know when a player has that special something. You were born to do this.'

Sergio jogged away with a huge smile on his face. He was ready.

Spain got off to a flying start, with two goals inside the first twenty minutes. That settled everyone down and they passed the ball around effortlessly. With all eyes on the Spanish midfielders' dazzling touches, there was plenty of room for Sergio to push forward. Again and again, he raced down the right wing to support the attack. The game finished 4–0 and the dressing room afterwards was buzzing.

'Great game today,' Iker said, patting Sergio on the back. 'You would never have guessed it was your first World Cup game.'

'That's the beauty of being a young player,' Raúl added. 'You just go out and play. You don't feel the pressure or have the bad memories that some of us old guys do!'

A 3–1 win over Tunisia kept Spain's momentum going and Sergio joined most of the other starters on the bench for the final group game against Saudi Arabia, with qualification already in the bag. Even that was a cool experience as he sat next to Xavi and Xabi Alonso and listened to them break down things in the game that he hadn't even noticed.

A powerhouse French team awaited them in the second round and it was hard not to feel a little intimidated. Sergio could remember watching Spain lose to France in the Euro 2000 quarter-finals. This time, though, *Les Bleus* had Thierry Henry up front, as well as Zidane pulling the strings as the playmaker. Sergio was both excited and a little anxious about trying to keep those two quiet.

Everything went according to plan for most of the first half. Early on, Sergio used his speed to beat Henry to the ball and clear the danger. He wasn't going to let anyone get past him without a fight. Then, in the twenty-eighth minute, David Villa put Spain ahead from the penalty spot. *1–0!*

'Come on!' Sergio screamed, punching the air with passion.

Just before half-time, however, France came powering back. Franck Ribéry beat the offside trap and then dribbled around Casillas. *1–1!*

In the second half, France pushed forward in search of a winning goal. Ribéry dribbled in off the right wing and crossed towards Eric Abidal at the back post, but Sergio stretched out his leg just in time to kick the ball away.

'Great defending!' Casillas clapped and cheered on his goal line.

Could Spain stay strong and win it? With ten minutes to go, Zidane curled a beautiful free kick towards Patrick Vieira at the back post. As he headed it goalwards, Sergio jumped up bravely to make the block, but he could only deflect the ball into his own net. *2–1 to France!*

Sergio's heart sank as he stood there gripping the goalpost. After all their hard work, was that game – and tournament – over for *La Roja*? Yes, it was – in injury time, Zidane scored a third on the counter-attack, while Sergio was up the other end, trying to equalise. Spain were out of the 2006 World Cup and were heading home.

At the final whistle, Sergio was devastated, but Zidane came over to comfort him.

'Hey, you should be really proud of your performance tonight,' his Real Madrid teammate told him. 'You'll be back in four years' time, I promise, and by then, you'll be the leader!'

Sergio tried his best to smile and look forward to that future. It took a few days for him to turn the page on the 2006 World Cup and refocus on Real Madrid. But by the time he was back on the training ground with the rest of the players, he felt great.

Despite catching the eye with his performances in
Germany, Sergio hadn't forgotten that he still had
work to do to prove himself at the Bernabéu.

By the end of the 2006/07 season, he had done
just that. Real Madrid and Barcelona finished the
season tied on seventy-six points, but Real clinched
the league title because they had a better head-to-
head record against their rivals. And Sergio had
played a key part in both legs of *El Clásico*.

At home at the Bernabéu, he raced down the right
wing and delivered a perfect cross to Raúl. *1–0!*

Then away at the Nou Camp, he out-jumped his
Spanish teammate Carles to score with a fantastic
flick header. *3–2!*

*Goooooooooooooooooooooaaaaaaaaaaaaaaaaaalllllllllllll
llllllllllllll!!!!!!!!!!!!!!!!!!!!*

So, Sergio had certainly earned his first taste of La
Liga glory and boy – did he enjoy the big celebrations
at the Bernabéu. Real's Galácticos played like
superstars and they partied like superstars too!

It had been a long season, but it was all worth it to
be able to hold that huge trophy in his hands. Sergio

still left manager Fabio Capello pulling his hair out a few times on the touchline because of badly timed tackles, but his manager was always quick to tell him to keep playing with his physical style.

Just to show it was no fluke, Real Madrid defended their title the following year. And this time, they were ahead of Barcelona by a massive eighteen points. By now, Sergio was one of their star players and a real fan favourite. That was because as well as winning lots of heroic headers and tackles at the back, he also loved to attack, scoring six goals a season. Not bad for a defender!

'Hearing them sing my name, just like they did at Sevilla, is an amazing feeling,' he told Miriam when she visited him. 'I'm one of them now. A true Madridista.'

'You've given them two straight championships,' she replied. 'I'd be singing your name too if I were a Real Madrid fan...'

Sergio gave her a jokey glare.

'...which I am, of course,' Miriam finished, laughing.

CHAPTER 11

EURO 2008: EXCITING NEW ERA

'Can you believe the boos?' Sergio asked, turning to Iker as they got changed after their last warm-up game before Euro 2008. 'We really need the fans to get behind us.'

'The fans are just so hungry for success at one of these tournaments,' Iker replied. 'I can't really blame them.'

Something felt different from the moment that Sergio joined up with his Spain teammates ahead of Euro 2008, to be hosted by Austria and Switzerland. He was still finding his way in international football, but he had already played enough times for his country to notice the more positive feeling around the squad.

El Sabio even lightened the training schedule, cancelling one session so that the players could have an afternoon off.

'Sergio, spread the word, we're having a video game tournament in my room,' Xavi announced. 'Sounds like we'll have nine or ten guys there.' Sergio thought back to the World Cup two years earlier and couldn't remember anything like that happening.

Ahead of Spain's first Euro 2008 game, El Sabio gathered the players in one of the hotel meeting rooms. 'We all know that other tournaments have ended badly for us. If people want to write us off, that's fine. Let them. This time, it's going to be different. We're here to win.'

Spain looked deadly up front with Fernando Torres partnering David Villa, and Xavi and Andrés Iniesta pulling the strings. 'If we can just keep things tight at the back, we'll be unstoppable going forward,' Sergio had told his friends before leaving for Austria. 'Whatever you do, don't make any plans for July.'

When the Spain bus arrived at the stadium for their first group game against Russia, Sergio could feel the nervous excitement building.

El Sabio gave the team their final instructions – 'Stick together, trust each other and be ruthless' – and Sergio joined in the high fives. 'Vamos!' the players screamed as they headed for the tunnel.

Playing at right-back, Sergio had countless chances to get forward and support the attack. If anything, he had to remind himself to stay back at times to avoid being caught out by quick Russian counter-attacks.

But once Spain got ahead, everyone could relax. Fernando raced onto a long pass and set up David for the first goal, and Sergio sprinted over to join the celebrations. 'Yes!!!'

David finished with a hat-trick, giving Spain the perfect start. The positive performance made the Spanish camp even more fun. 'Remember how we'd all just stick in small groups or stay in our own rooms at other tournaments?' Iker said one evening. 'Now, we've got most of the squad packed into one hotel room and it feels like we're all one big family!'

Spain picked up a second victory against Sweden, but this one felt a little sourer for Sergio. In the first half, he chased back to reach a dangerous through-ball but was muscled off the ball by Zlatan Ibrahimović for Sweden's equaliser. Sergio picked himself up off the floor, looked hopefully for a whistle or an assistant referee's flag, and then hung his head in disappointment.

'Brush it off, mate,' Iker called out. 'We'll just get another goal.'

David rescued Sergio with a last-minute winner, but that was not the end of it. El Sabio took Sergio aside at the next training session to deliver a bit of a wake-up call.

'Sergio, you're a huge part of this team but I need to see more focus. That doesn't just mean being in the right place on the pitch. It's also about showing up on time for meetings and doing all the little things that contribute to winning.'

Sergio was shocked – he knew he should have done better on the Sweden goal, but he had not realised that other factors were frustrating El Sabio.

He nodded, and El Sabio put an arm round his shoulder, eager not to leave Sergio too shaken.

'Message received,' Sergio replied. 'I'm desperate to win and I'll work even harder to help us bring home the trophy.'

Sergio had a few days to think things over as El Sabio rested his first-teamers in the final group game, with qualification already secured, but he was back for a tense quarter-final against Italy. As the match went to penalties, Sergio took a deep breath. He was not going to be one of the five penalty takers, but he might be called upon if it went to sudden death. He could barely watch as he lined up along the halfway line with his teammates. 'Come on, Iker!' he muttered under his breath.

It was a rollercoaster of emotions – joy as Iker saved one penalty, agony as Dani missed, then the joy of Iker making another big save. As Cesc Fàbregas stepped forward to take Spain's fifth penalty, Sergio screamed encouragement. The penalty flew into the net. Shootouts had been cruel to the Spaniards in the past – but maybe this was a sign that things were about to change.

Sergio sprinted over to Iker as most of the players ran to Cesc, then they all gathered in one big huddle to celebrate. 'Two more to go!' they chanted.

'We'll have to play better if we're going to beat Russia in the semi-finals,' El Sabio reminded his players. 'But enjoy this moment – we've certainly waited long enough to win a shootout! I'm proud of you guys.'

Sergio knew that the Russians would make a fast start, spurred on by the loss to Spain earlier in the tournament. El Sabio had talked a lot over the last few days about getting through the first fifteen minutes of a game without taking too many risks. Mission accomplished – against the Russian team, they got to half-time at 0–0, but would have to finish the job without David, who had limped off.

Once Xavi scored early in the second half, Russia never looked like recovering. Fernando almost doubled the lead from Sergio's cross, and Spain cruised to a 3–0 win. Back in the dressing room, there was some singing and plenty of hugging, but they all knew that the job wasn't done yet.

'The trophy is within reach now, boys,' Iker said as they all sat at their lockers. 'We need ninety more top quality minutes if we're going to beat Germany in the final.'

Before he knew it, Sergio was on the bus on the way to the final. As some of his teammates headed out for the warm-up, he grabbed a marker pen and prepared a message for his white undershirt. If he was going to be celebrating at the final whistle, he wanted everyone to know that Antonio was there in his thoughts. His good friend from Sevilla had died a year ago and Sergio still missed him. He would never forget Antonio and all the moments they had shared along the way.

El Sabio called for quiet and looked around the dressing room. 'Our country has waited years for a champion, and you have the chance to be part of history today,' he said, almost shouting. 'But the only way to do that is through togetherness. We're better than them man-for-man – I believe that, and you should too. But it's teamwork and courage that will get us over the line tonight.'

Those words had the right effect on Sergio. He was ready to run through a wall for his manager. He pulled up his socks, re-tied his boots and did a lap of the dressing room, high-fiving his teammates. As he stood in the tunnel, he pictured what it would be like to parade through the streets of Madrid if they won. Then he quickly snapped out of it. He was thinking too far ahead – and Germany were fearsome opponents.

Sergio sang the anthem loudly and proudly. His dad's words from earlier that day echoed in his mind. 'I know it's a huge moment in your career but try to enjoy it. I hope it isn't your only final for Spain, but it could be. Take it all in.'

He looked to his left and then to his right, and he saw large sections of red in the crowd. We're going to need the fans to push us along today, he thought.

Sergio saved his best game of the tournament for

the final. He had expected to be battling through aches and pains, but instead he felt fresh. While always making sure he didn't leave Carles stranded, he burst forward at every opportunity. Halfway through the first half, Sergio played the ball up the line to Cesc and then raced up in support. Cesc laid the ball back and Sergio clipped a perfect cross towards Fernando, whose header bounced back off the post.

Sergio jumped in the air expecting to see the ball end up in the net but could only put his head in his hands and run back to his position.

Fernando was more clinical ten minutes later, clipping the ball into the German net from Xavi's cross. *1–0 to Spain!*

'I was cursing you ten minutes ago but you're my hero again now,' Sergio joked as he hugged Fernando and jogged back to the halfway line.

'Keep the ball, keep the ball,' Xavi called as he floated around the pitch. Whenever Sergio was under pressure, Xavi was there for a quick pass. He never wastes a pass, Sergio thought to himself for the hundredth time that month.

Spain won a free kick midway through the second half, and Sergio looked to Carles to see who was going up for it. 'You go,' Carles replied.

Sergio drifted towards the back post and looked across to make sure he stayed onside. Xavi whipped the ball in and Sergio's eyes lit up. It was coming straight to him and he was unmarked. He watched it all the way and then powered a header towards the top corner. He looked up to see the German keeper tip the ball away at full stretch.

So close! The sea of red shirts behind the goal had jumped out of their seats ready to celebrate.

'I should have gone for the other corner,' he said to Xavi as he sprinted back, shaking his head.

Spain wasted a couple more chances, setting up a nervous last few minutes. Sergio never stopped running. He was still bursting towards the German box in the dying minutes, even as El Sabio was out on the touchline urging his team to stay calm.

Deep in stoppage time, Iker blasted a free kick up the pitch and the referee blew the final whistle. Spain were the new European Champions! Sergio rushed to his teammates as they hugged, jumped, screamed and sang. It was a summer he would never forget – and, for Spain, it was really just the beginning.

Campeones, Campeones, Olé, Olé, Olé!

CHAPTER 12

LOSING BATTLES WITH BARCELONA

'Turn it off,' Sergio called to René as they sat in his living room, watching Barcelona celebrate with the Champions League trophy. Red and blue confetti was scattered on the pitch and the players were halfway through a victory lap. 'I can't watch any more of this.'

René knew better than to argue. He reached for the remote and the room went quiet. Sergio stared at the floor.

'Don't get me wrong,' he said eventually. 'I'm happy for Xavi and Andrés. I love those guys. But all anyone wants to talk about is Barcelona. What about Real Madrid? People are forgetting all about us.'

It had been a tough year for the Galácticos. When they won La Liga in 2007 and 2008, all the talk was about Real Madrid. But they had been blown away by Barcelona during the 2008/09 season. Led by Lionel Messi, Barcelona had now landed the Treble. Guardiola, Sergio's old Olympics hero, had made history in his first season as Barcelona boss.

'We should all be watching this and getting angry,' Sergio said. 'If we need a reason to be doing extra training and fighting even harder, this is it. Barcelona have raised the bar. Now we have to respond. We better get things right next season, or the fans are going to be fuming.'

It didn't help that Real Madrid had been changing managers so regularly. Bernd Schuster was in charge for less than two seasons, then Juande Ramos lasted just six months. Now it was Manuel Pellegrini's turn.

As Sergio looked around the pitch during pre-season training, he was confident that Real Madrid had a squad capable of battling Barcelona all the way. They had top new players in every position: Raúl Albiol and Álvaro Arbeloa in defence, Xabi Alonso

and Kaká in midfield, and Karim Benzema and
Cristiano Ronaldo in attack.

The new Galácticos were ready to bounce back,
and the early signs were good:

Real Madrid	*3–2*	*Deportivo de La Coruña*
Espanyol	*0–3*	*Real Madrid*
Real Madrid	*5–0*	*Xerez*
Villarreal	*0–2*	*Real Madrid*
Real Madrid	*3–0*	*Tenerife...*

'We've won five out of five, we're scoring goals for
fun and we're keeping it tight at the back,' Sergio
told his parents one night. 'This is exactly the
response we needed.'

But Barcelona were always looming. When it
came to head-to-head battles, they always seemed
to have the edge. Sergio was up all night wondering
how Real Madrid had lost at the Nou Camp when
Barcelona played most of the second half with ten
men. It got worse when Barcelona won 2–0 at
the Bernabéu late in the season, with the Real

Madrid fans jeering Sergio and his teammates at the final whistle. Guardiola's men won the title by just three points.

'We can't beat them,' Sergio said to Iker, throwing his arms up in the air in frustration. They had also been through the pain of an early Champions League exit. 'That's another season without one of the big trophies. Now what? Another coaching change? No wonder the fans are booing us.'

Iker shook his head. 'I know, it's a rough spell for us at the moment. But you've just got to be patient – we all have to be patient. Our time will come again. We pushed Barcelona all the way in the title race. If the ball had bounced our way a couple more times, we'd be celebrating with the trophy now.'

'I know,' Sergio said, but he was still on edge. Iker got up to leave, thinking the conversation was over, but Sergio kept going: 'We have to stop trying to beat them at their own pretty passing game. It's not the Real Madrid way but maybe we have to be more physical and get in their heads. The trouble is, we're friends with half of their team!'

Iker laughed. 'Well, let's keep it that way. We're going to be travelling together to South Africa next week, so put your mind games on pause! Let's go and win the World Cup instead.'

CHAPTER 13

ON TOP OF THE WORLD

Sergio saw immediately that, after their success
at Euro 2008, people were talking about Spain
differently. For years, they had been the dark horses.
Now, with the 2010 World Cup looming, they were
being talked about among the favourites.

'That was just for starters,' Sergio told his mum as
he packed his bag ready for the tournament in South
Africa. 'We've got basically the same team and I
don't think anyone, or anything, can stop us.'

He saw himself differently too. He had grown
up a lot in the past two years and felt like a better
defender and a better professional.

Spain were drawn in Group H alongside
Switzerland, Honduras and Chile.

A nightmare start – a 1–0 loss to the Swiss –
proved to be a wake-up call. 'Well, if you thought life
would be easy as European champions, there's your
answer,' said manager Vicente del Bosque,
aka *El Mister,* to the shocked Spanish players in a
very quiet dressing room. He was facing the tough
task of following on from Aragonés's success at
Euro 2008. 'But there's still time to put things right.
We'll go over the film tomorrow and see what we
need to fix. Let's make sure we're sharper against
Honduras.'

Sergio was especially disappointed. He was one
of the last to shower and get dressed afterwards. He
knew Spain were much better than they had shown
in that first game.

His dad called his hotel room that night to try
to cheer him up. 'It's early days, son. I've watched
enough of these tournaments to know that it's never
over after one game.'

'We were terrible,' Sergio replied, with no energy

at all. 'That World Cup trophy feels a long way away right now.'

'You're talking like you're out of the tournament. Take it one game at a time. Go and win the next one.'

By the time the next game finally arrived, Sergio felt calmer and he wanted to make sure his teammates felt the same way. Luckily, he had a plan. He spoke to Iker that morning and explained what he needed him to do.

Two hours before kick-off against Honduras, as the players settled into their dressing room, Iker stood on a chair and waved his arms. 'Listen up, everyone. To help us get in the zone for today's match, we have a special guest DJ.'

Sergio peered through the doorway and saw Xavi, Andrés and Fernando looking at each other with confused faces. They were probably expecting a famous Spanish DJ, he thought, giggling to himself.

'Put your hands together for DJ Rockin' Ramos,' Iker announced.

Sergio put his sunglasses on and hit PLAY on his

music player. Music blared from the speakers tucked under his arm. He walked in and the dressing room erupted into cheers and laughter.

Iker high-fived him, while Sergio set up the speakers on the table in the middle of the room, and then asked, 'Who's ready for some classic Spanish tunes?' in his best DJ voice.

For some time, Sergio had been unofficially in charge of the music selection in the dressing room and on the bus. He hoped his little performance had taken some of the tension out of the pre-game build-up.

It seemed to work. Spain won 2–0 and the victory could have been even bigger. Sergio took every chance to get forward, seeing that Honduras posed little threat on the counter-attack. 'We were much better today,' he said to Iker as they walked back to the bus. 'Did you see the guy push me over in the box at that corner? We should have had two penalties. If the group comes down to goal difference, we might regret some of our misses, but we looked more like ourselves.'

'Yeah, I could probably have had a cup of tea and a picnic in the box tonight,' Iker replied. 'You guys didn't let them get near our goal.'

'If we take care of business against Chile, that sloppy start will be forgotten,' Sergio said.

Goals from David and Andrés were enough to sink Chile and put Spain top of Group H. That meant a matchup with Cristiano and Portugal in the next round. 'Get in!' Sergio shouted at the final whistle. 'We're back on track.' He never got tired of seeing the way David, Xavi and Andrés worked the ball around the pitch, even in the tightest spaces. 'Those guys give us a chance against anyone,' he had told René that morning.

As the bus pulled into the hotel where the Spanish squad was staying, Sergio's phone buzzed. It was a text from Cristiano. 'I'll try not to embarrass you too badly, but I can't promise anything!!'

Sergio laughed. Typical Cristiano. 'Make sure you bring your shin pads!' he wrote back.

Beneath all the jokes, Sergio knew the game against Portugal was going to be a tough battle and

a game where he had to make defending the top
priority. Vicente had a similar message. 'Normally,
I'd say push up and give us that width on the right.
But Cristiano is a different challenge. We can't leave
that kind of space for him to hurt us.'

But with Cristiano spending more of his time on
the other wing, the game plan changed a little. 'If
he's on the other wing, we've got enough cover,'
Vicente called as Sergio walked over to take a throw-
in. 'You can be more aggressive in supporting the
midfield.'

Sergio didn't need to be told twice. He pushed up,
giving Andrés, Xabi and Xavi an outlet pass. With
thirty minutes to go, he got the ball on the touchline,
took a quick touch and swung in a dipping cross. It
was perfect for Fernando, but his header was well
saved. 'It's coming, boys,' Sergio shouted, with his
hands still on his head after the near miss. Minutes
later, David smashed the ball home after a quick-fire
move. *1–0 to Spain!*

Sergio almost added a second goal late on with
another burst down the right, hitting the ball as

sweetly as ever, but denied by another excellent save. 'Oh, come on!' he yelled.

'That's your one good shot for the tournament gone,' Andrés called, laughing.

The next round brought another narrow win in a tournament full of low-scoring games. 'We're not making things easy for ourselves,' Sergio said to Miriam on their evening call after the 1–0 quarter-final win over Paraguay. 'Thank goodness for Iker. What a penalty save!'

'But we should have had a penalty too,' René reminded him. 'Anyway, all that matters is that we have a World Cup semi-final to look forward to now. Germany will be out for revenge after the Euro 2008 final.'

The build-up to the semi-final was eventful, with Carles trying to fight off an injury and Sergio wondering if he would have to shift over to centre-back. 'I'll do whatever El Mister needs me to do, but we need Puyi,' Sergio said to Iker as they waited for the news. 'I've learned so much from him over the past two tournaments.'

In the end, Carles was fit to start, giving Spain a big boost. 'We know how this tournament has gone,' El Mister said. 'Lots of cautious football and not many goals. When we get a chance, we've got to be ruthless. You know the Germans will be.'

El Mister's words rang true. Spain had plenty of the ball and passed it well, but it was 0–0 heading into the final twenty minutes. 'We just need one chance,' Sergio said to Carles as they waited for a German substitution.

Though Spain's midfield stars were small, they had four tall defenders capable of scoring from set-pieces. As Xavi put the ball down by the corner flag, Sergio joined Carles, Gerard Piqué and Joan in the box. Sergio made his burst towards the back post but saw instantly that the ball would not reach him. Instead, Carles came flying in and thumped a header into the net. *1–0 to Spain!*

'Puyi! What a header!' he screamed, chasing after him.

'World Cup final!' Sergio yelled as the final whistle sounded. Once again, one goal was enough for Spain.

The players hugged, the substitutes ran on to join in and Sergio could hear the fans going wild.

'Another clean sheet,' Iker said, patting Sergio on the back. 'One more of those and we could be world champs!'

Sergio had played in some big games, but the World Cup Final was on a whole other level. Only the Netherlands stood in their way, and Sergio knew all about their threats – Arjen Robben and Robin van Persie, in particular.

'To get this far and not lift the trophy would be too painful,' Sergio said, pacing his room while talking to Jesús Navas, who was now a regular in the Spain squad. 'We have to win.'

As they walked onto the pitch for the national anthems, they went past the glistening World Cup trophy. Sergio took a long look at the prize. 'We'll be back for you later,' he called out. He had stood with his teammates for the Spanish national anthem countless times, but this one was extra-special. The hairs stood up on his arms and the back of his neck.

The Dutch game plan was clearly to unsettle Spain

with a physical style of play. From the start, there were little trips and kicks. Sergio was one of the first to appeal to the referee when he saw Xabi hit the ground after a dangerous high foot. 'This is getting out of hand,' he said to Andrés after yet another foul.

Still, Spain just couldn't score – not in ninety minutes and not in 105 minutes. Sergio willed his body to keep moving as they entered the final five minutes of extra time. Then it happened. Sergio saw Jesús pick up the ball just in front of him and start a mazy dribble. Tired Dutch defenders struggled to keep up. The ball fell to Andrés in midfield, then out to Fernando on the left. 'Put it in the box,' Sergio yelled. Fernando's cross was only half-cleared, and the ball was scrambled through to Andrés. 'Shoot!' Sergio called, praying that this was the big moment. Andrés pulled back his right foot and rocketed in a low shot. *1–0!*

Sergio leapt in the air as he saw the net bulge. Everything else was a blur, from sprinting the length of the pitch, to joining the celebrations to surviving the remaining minutes. And then it was over. The

Dutch players threw themselves to the floor while Spain jumped for joy.

Climbing the steps to receive his medal took every last ounce of Sergio's energy, but it was an amazing moment that he would never forget. He was a world champion!

'I love this team,' he thought to himself as they posed for photos and sang with the fans.

Campeones, Campeones, Olé, Olé, Olé!

CHAPTER 14

THE MISKICK AND
THE TRUCE

25 April 2012, Estadio Santiago Bernabéu, Madrid

Sergio carefully placed the ball on the penalty spot.
The Real Madrid fans fell silent, giving him a chance
to focus. He took a quick glance at Manuel Neuer
in the Bayern goal, charged in and struck the ball as
hard as he could. As soon as Sergio made contact,
he knew he was heading for disaster. He watched in
agony as the ball sailed high over the bar.

He turned angrily to look at the penalty spot, as if
it had somehow propelled the ball so high. It was an
ugly miss and he just couldn't believe it as he walked
slowly back to the halfway line. The crowd was in

shock. Thirty seconds later, the travelling Bayern fans were jumping around as they scored the winning penalty and clinched their place in the Champions League final.

Sergio was one of three Real Madrid players to miss in the shootout, and the other players and coaches tried their best to console him. But it really stung. After all the high points during the season, he felt like he had let everyone down.

He didn't want to talk about it either. He put a towel over his head and sat next to his locker. Meanwhile, he could hear the Bayern celebrations down the corridor.

Even winning La Liga a few weeks later could only slightly ease Sergio's pain of that penalty miss. Every time he thought he had moved on, it would pop up and upset him.

But the penalty miss wasn't the only thing on his mind when he came in to clear out his locker for the summer. As he and Iker sat down for lunch in the Real Madrid cafeteria, Sergio looked over his shoulder to check that they were alone and that there was no chance of manager José Mourinho walking in.

'This must be top secret stuff,' Iker replied. 'Wait, you're not being sold, are you?'

'No, nothing like that,' Sergio said, but his face stayed serious. 'We need to talk about this rivalry with Barcelona. It's getting out of hand. We have good friends on that team and there seems to be a red card every time we play them.'

Iker nodded. 'I know – and I think I can guess where you're going with this. We had some ugly games this season.'

It was Sergio's turn to nod. 'We're on the same page. How are we going to win Euro 2012 if we're not speaking to each other? We need to talk to Xavi and Andrés.'

'Do you think they'll pick up the call?'

'Come on, of course. We've been friends for years. I bet they are thinking the same thing that we are.'

With the room still quiet, Sergio took out his phone, dialled Xavi's number and hit the speakerphone button.

'Hey, man. It's Sergio and Iker. Listen, we were just talking about what a rough season this has been.

We're going to be on the same team at Euro 2012 and I think we need to clear the air.'

'I know,' Xavi said. 'We've been saying the same thing. I know it's an intense battle whenever Barcelona and Real Madrid play, but our friendship shouldn't get lost in that.'

'I'm really sorry for my role in the arguments,' Iker jumped in.

'Me too,' Sergio said.

'Thanks, guys. That means a lot. I know I got too fired up in one of the games as well. Let's start afresh when we meet up with the squad. We can forget all the nastiness of this season and focus on winning for Spain.'

'Awesome!' Sergio replied. 'Will you talk to Andrés too? We'll talk to the other Spanish boys here.'

'Cool, yes, I'll spread the word too. I think everyone will be glad not to turn up and be sitting on opposite sides of the room!'

They all laughed, mostly with relief.

'See you in a few weeks then,' Sergio said. 'Let's bring another trophy home.'

CHAPTER 15

EURO 2012: PLAYING IT COOL

By now, Sergio knew exactly what to bring for the big tournaments, and he expected to be at Euro 2012 all the way through to the final. As he was unpacking his suitcase, there was a knock at the door.

It was Iker.

'Seriously, you're still unpacking?' he said. 'I've never seen anyone take so long! Creams, hair gel, hand lotion – did you leave anything in your bathroom at home?'

Sergio laughed. 'Hey, some of us like to look our best for the cameras! What's wrong with that?'

Iker ignored that one. 'I'll wait for you and we can head down to the meeting together.'

He sat on the edge of the bed while Sergio found hangers for his last few T-shirts. 'We're on a mission to make history. Have you seen all the reports about that?'

'Yeah, they're everywhere at the moment,' Sergio replied. 'No team has ever won three in a row before. It would be pretty special to have six years at the top like that.'

'I really think we can do it, especially now that the team spirit has been repaired. We know how to pace ourselves and play our best football in the knockout rounds.'

All of that proved to be true as La Roja surged through to the semi-final against Portugal. It was the same old Spain, even if their defence was slightly different. Carles had injured his knee just weeks before the start of the tournament, and so Sergio had switched from right-back to centre-back, the position he usually played for Real Madrid. He was really enjoying his new role alongside Gerard at the heart of the backline.

Now, however, Sergio was facing another test

of his nerves. The semi-final had finished goalless after extra time, which only meant one thing: a penalty shootout. Just a couple of months after his penalty heartbreak against Bayern, Sergio had a choice to make – sit it out or put himself in the spotlight again.

El Mister and his coaching staff were writing out the names of the five Spanish penalty takers and checking on any possible injuries that might affect the order. When it came to Sergio, El Mister just wanted to be sure.

'Sergio, what do you think? Still feeling confident?'

Sergio had already made his decision. He was not a quitter. 'One hundred per cent!'

'Okay, great. You've got the fourth penalty.'

When Sergio's turn came, there had already been two misses, one for each team, and the shootout was deadlocked at 2–2. He had the chance to put Spain back in front. 'Good luck, pal,' Andrés said quietly as Sergio started the long walk from the halfway line.

Sergio placed the ball on the spot and took a deep
breath. He knew exactly what he was going to do, and
he had practised it again and again over the past week.
Now he just had to get it right under pressure. He
took eight steps back and then began his run up. At
the last second, he pulled back from blasting his shot
and just gave the ball the softest clip straight down
the middle. As the Portugal keeper dived to his left,
Sergio's penalty floated softly into the net.

'Vamooooooooos!' Sergio shouted, pointing to the
Spain badge on his shirt.

He jogged back and rejoined his teammates on the
halfway line.

'What a show-off!' teased Cesc. 'It takes nerves of
steel to do that in a big semi-final.'

'Well, it turns out that hitting penalties as hard
as I can doesn't end well for me!' Sergio replied,
laughing.

Now they turned and begged Iker to come up with
a big stop. Bruno Alves ran forward for Portugal's
fourth penalty and his shot cannoned back off the bar.

That meant Cesc had the chance to win it. 'Come

on, come on, come on,' Sergio whispered under his breath. Cesc's shot went low to the left, and the keeper anticipated that correctly, but the ball hit the inside of the post and rolled into the opposite corner. Spain were in yet another final!

Cesc ran to Iker and the whole squad followed.

As Sergio walked back to the dressing room, he thought back to his Champions League penalty. It was a cruel way to decide games, but he was proud of himself for not shying away from it.

'A lot of players would have hidden in that moment,' El Mister told Sergio the next morning. 'Instead, you ran towards it. I haven't seen many more confident penalties than that one!'

'I'll always put my hand up for that kind of thing,' Sergio said, shrugging. 'The more pressure, the better. Bring it on.'

Sergio had heard some neutrals moaning about Spain being in another big final, but they had won games the easy way and the hard way, all while conceding just one goal. He took particular pride in that.

Spain had struggled to score goals during the tournament, but in the final they attacked Italy like a team that had been hiding those talents all along. Xavi and Andrés were everywhere. Sergio loved to watch that duo on top form. It was 2–0 at half-time and the Italians had barely had the ball. 'Don't relax, guys,' Sergio called out in the dressing room, sensing that his teammates were taking their foot off the gas. 'Let's keep the ball and get a third goal.'

The second half drifted along, and Sergio kept one eye on the clock on the scoreboard. Italy were running out of time and, as they sent more players forward, Spain put the finishing touches on another tournament victory. Fernando and Juan Mata, both on as subs, scored in the final ten minutes as Sergio got ready for yet another international victory lap.

As Iker lifted the trophy high above his head and Sergio jumped up and down with one arm around Xavi, the tension from the battles against Barcelona was the furthest thing from any of their minds. Spain had won their third straight major tournament. 'I'm not done yet,' Sergio told René as the players met up with their families. 'Now we've got to make it four in a row.'

René rolled his eyes and smiled. 'All that can wait. At least give yourself a few hours to savour this one. Come on, follow me. Mum and Dad are waiting to see the medal.'

CHAPTER 16

PILAR

Just like after the glory at Euro 2008 and the 2010 World Cup, Sergio and his teammates celebrated their Euro 2012 success in style with a huge party back in Spain. As he walked into the room in his best suit, he had no idea that it was a night that would change his life.

First, he had some familiar faces to catch up with. He shook hands with old friends, former teammates and former coaches. There was a smile on every face. 'Viva España!' one of them shouted.

Across the room, he spotted Ivan, a TV presenter who he knew well from covering games with both Real Madrid and Spain. Ivan waved, and Sergio picked up his drink and walked over to catch up.

'I haven't seen you in months,' he said, giving Ivan a big hug.

'That's what happens when you're busy being famous and winning tournaments, I guess,' Ivan replied, along with a playful punch on the arm. 'By the way, we all loved that penalty!'

'Thanks,' Sergio said, laughing. 'If I'd messed it up, I would have been so embarrassed. It was a crazy summer – again – but it's good to be back and have a few weeks to go on holiday and...'

But Sergio didn't finish his sentence. Suddenly he was lost for words. A woman appeared next to Ivan with a drink in each hand. Sergio recognised her straight away.

Ivan turned, and took his drink. 'Thanks, Pilar. Cheers!' He paused. 'You've met Pilar before, right?'

Sergio shook his head. 'No. We've probably been at the same party a few times but we've never been introduced. I'm Sergio.'

He put out his hand and Pilar shook it.

'I know who you are!' she said, giggling. 'We've

all been watching you guys for the past month. Congratulations!'

Sergio went a bit red but recovered quickly. 'Thanks! I was just starting to tell Ivan that all I want to do now is sit on a beach for a few weeks.'

'Weren't you doing that in between the games at the Euros? All you had to do was play for ninety minutes and then you got three days off. I wish my job worked like that.'

Sergio was about to argue when he saw in her eyes that she was teasing him. She grinned, and he grinned back. 'You almost got me with that one,' he said.

Ivan's phone buzzed. He mouthed 'Sorry' and disappeared towards a quieter spot.

'Are you working tonight or are you just here for the party?' he asked. Pilar was a TV presenter and one of the most well-known women in the country.

'No work for me tonight,' she said. 'I'm meeting up with a couple of friends, but they're running late, so you've got me all to yourself for now.'

Sergio smiled. The more he talked to Pilar, the

more he felt a connection. The way she laughed took his breath away.

It turned out they had a lot in common, and Pilar spent most months in Madrid. Sergio really hoped that meant he might see her again in the weeks ahead.

Suddenly Pilar waved across the room. Her friends had arrived.

'Give me your phone for a minute,' she said.

Sergio handed it over hesitantly and watched as Pilar pressed a few different buttons. He hoped this wasn't some kind of joke.

'There you go,' she said, passing the phone back. 'My number is in there now. Give me a call if you want some company for your relaxing summer plans.' She gave him a kiss on the cheek and disappeared through the crowded room.

Sergio watched her go.

'I bet you're happy you came to the party now,' a voice said from behind him.

He turned to see Ivan looking very proud of himself.

'She's amazing,' Sergio said. 'I really want to see her again. This could be the start of something great.'

Soon, Sergio and Pilar were inseparable – long walks, fancy dinners and quiet nights in front of the TV. In no time at all, it felt like Pilar had been part of his life for years.

'I can't wait to see what's next for us,' he told Paqui that summer. 'I think she's the one.'

CHAPTER 17

LA DÉCIMA

'This is it, boys,' Sergio called, as the Real Madrid players filtered out towards the tunnel. 'Dig in for ninety minutes and we'll be back where we belong – in the Champions League final.'

'*La Décima*!' they all shouted. Real Madrid had been chasing their tenth European crown for years. If they could hold onto their 1–0 first leg lead against Bayern Munich, *La Décima!* would be at their fingertips.

As Sergio passed the ball back and forth with Luka and Pepe, he could feel the noise from the Bayern fans getting louder.

'Take no chances early on,' he reminded them. 'If

they get off to a fast start, this place will be rocking.'

Sergio did his best to set the tone, sticking tightly to Bayern strikers Mario Mandžukić and Thomas Müller. 'Don't let them get comfortable,' Real's latest manager Carlo Ancelotti had said again and again during the week.

As Real Madrid started to settle, they won a corner on the far side, and Sergio jogged forward. As usual, the penalty area was packed so he took a few steps out towards the edge of the box. Jinking one way, then the other, he tried to create some space to attack the cross. From his earliest days with Camas, he had been an expert at being in the right place at the right time for crosses.

Sergio spun away from his marker just as Luka swung the corner in and instantly saw it was a perfect ball. He just had to make the right connection. He timed his jump well and powered a header towards the goal. No goalkeeper could save that.

Gooooooooooooooooooooaaaaaaaaaaaaaaaaalllllllllllll llllllllllllll!!!!!!!!!!!!!!!!!!!!

Sergio sprinted off to celebrate and slid on his

knees near the corner flag. His teammates were
chasing after him in a flash. 'You little beauty!' Karim
screamed in his ear.

'We've got to finish the job now!' Sergio replied,
patting the Real Madrid badge on his shirt.

A few minutes later, Gareth Bale won a free kick
in a dangerous position and Sergio was back in the
Bayern box. Sergio signalled for Pepe to come over
and whispered, 'Make the near post run – it might
end up being a decoy, but you'll clear space for the
rest of us.'

When he saw Pepe dart towards the near post,
Sergio pulled behind him. Once again, the ball in
was a good one. Sergio saw Pepe leap and get a little
flick. There was no time to think – his instincts took
over. He dived forward to where he thought the ball
would land and timed it perfectly to guide a header
into the net.

*Goooooooooooooooooooaaaaaaaaaaaaaaaaaalllllllllllll
lllllllllllllll!!!!!!!!!!!!!!!!!!!*

This one meant even more. Now the final really
felt within reach.

'Vamoooooooooooos!' Sergio yelled, pumping his fists. He couldn't believe he had scored two goals in a Champions League semi-final.

'You're a natural goalscorer,' Cristiano said, hugging Sergio.

'You guys have such an easy job,' Sergio joked. 'Just give me two chances and I'll score two goals.'

Cristiano scored a third before half-time and the Real Madrid dressing room was full of excitement. 'Don't lose your focus,' Carlo said, trying to keep his players grounded. 'Crazy things can happen if you start thinking the game is over. I'm sure you all remember my AC Milan team that was winning 3–0 at half-time and lost the 2005 final.'

With Sergio winning every header and every tackle, Bayern had no way back, and later on Cristiano completed a special night, making it 4–0.

Even having won so many big games, this one meant a lot. 'I'm going to remember this night for a long time,' Sergio told Luka. 'We ripped them apart.'

Luka grinned. 'You always save your best games for when we need them the most. When you scored the first goal, I knew we were going to be fine.'

'The biggest test is still to come,' Carlo warned. 'If we want *La Décima*, we will have to fight to the final second. But all that can wait. For now, let's enjoy tonight.'

The next three weeks went by slower than ever for Sergio. The final weeks of the La Liga ticked by and then it was all about the Champions League final – in Lisbon against cross-city rivals Atlético Madrid.

By the time he walked into the hotel meeting room for the team's final preparations, the semi-final victory felt like a whole season ago. 'We can't blow this chance,' he had told René on the phone that morning. 'We haven't won the Champions League for twelve years. For a giant club like this, that's unacceptable.'

Once all the players had grabbed some water and found a seat, Carlo went over the game plan. 'We know Atlético well, and they know us. This is going to be a tight, physical game and we have to stay calm. Atlético will pack the midfield and force us to beat them on the wings. Be direct.'

Sergio heard those words in his head again as he
walked out onto the pitch for the final, with the
Champions League anthem welcoming the teams.
That always gave him goosebumps.

Ten minutes before half-time, disaster struck for
Real Madrid. Atlético looped a ball back into the box,
Iker started to come out for it, then stopped, and
Atlético defender Diego Godin headed the ball into
the net. Sergio kicked the turf in anger.

The minutes ticked by in the second half. Sergio
clapped his hands to encourage his teammates and
did his best to drive forward with the ball when
Atlético sat back. He partly wished he was playing at
right-back so he could get forward more.

Gareth fired two shots wide, Cristiano mistimed
his jump for a header from Sergio's cross, and Isco
missed the target from just outside the box. The
prospect of *La Décima* was slipping away. 'There's
still time,' Sergio called to his teammates.

Deep into stoppage time, Real Madrid won a
corner on the right. Luka placed the ball by the
corner flag and took a deep breath. He had a quick

look at where he wanted to land the cross. Sergio jumped on the spot, getting ready to attack the ball if it came near him. Atlético defenders were grabbing shirts and doing everything possible to deny a clean header.

It was now or never. Sergio made a sharp run and got in front of his marker. The ball was perfect. He rose, almost in slow motion, and headed the ball down towards the corner and past the keeper's desperate dive.

Goooooooooooooooooooaaaaaaaaaaaaaaaallllllllllll llllllllllllll!!!!!!!!!!!!!!!!!!!!

Sergio had done it again.

The Real Madrid fans were on their feet – hugging and cheering. Sergio threw himself on the ground near the corner flag and his teammates dived on top. Even the substitutes were running over to celebrate with the hero of the hour.

'You're a lifesaver, man,' Cristiano said. 'What a header!'

'We're not leaving here without *La Décima*,' Sergio answered. He was so fired up that he felt dizzy.

He looked back at the Atlético players, who were picking themselves up off the ground. His joy was their heartbreak.

Carlo huddled the players together on the pitch as they prepared for extra time. There could surely only be one winner now, given Real Madrid's momentum. 'They're on the ropes and probably still in shock,' said Carlo. 'Play direct and run at them. There are going to be some tired legs out there.'

Sergio could see something was bothering Gareth. He walked over and put his hand on his shoulder. 'What's up, mate?'

'I can't hit the target today,' Gareth said, shaking his head. 'The game would be over if I'd taken my chances.'

'Come on, man. Don't worry about that. You're getting into the right positions and we all believe in you. Just focus on the next chance.'

Real Madrid were flying again. Luka raced forward but his shot was easily saved. Meanwhile, Cristiano had had a quiet game, but was now livening up.

'Keep attacking!' Sergio shouted, clapping his

hands. 'Another goal is coming. I can feel it.'

He was right. Ángel Di María weaved in and out of back-pedalling defenders and his cross looped up to the back post where Gareth jumped highest to head the ball into the top corner.

'What a comeback!' Sergio yelled as he ran over to celebrate. He jumped on Gareth's back. 'I knew you'd get the next one!' he shouted.

Marcelo smashed in a third goal for Real Madrid, and Sergio could see what it all meant to the fans. Then it was Cristiano's turn. He dribbled into the box, pushed the ball away from two defenders and was tripped. Penalty!

'This will just be the icing on the cake,' Sergio said, turning to Pepe as Cristiano stepped up to the spot. 'What a night!'

Cristiano drilled home the penalty and now it really was party time. Sergio sprinted across the pitch to join the celebrations by the corner flag. '*Olé olé, olé, olé,*' sang the Real Madrid fans.

Carlo embraced each of his players at the final whistle but saved his biggest hug for Sergio. 'Big players step up in big moments. You were a beast tonight.'

Sergio smiled. It was easily the most important goal he had ever scored.

As he walked over to high-five the rest of his teammates, he stopped to console the Atlético players who had seen their dream crushed. 'Neither team deserved to lose tonight,' he said. 'You guys had a great season. Be proud.'

One of the Real Madrid coaches suddenly appeared with a pile of T-shirts and started handing them out. Sergio unfolded his and saw a big Number 10 on the front – a special way to mark *La Décima* in all the photos with the trophy.

When it was Sergio's turned to hold the trophy, he took a long look at it. It had been a long quest, but he was finally a Champions League winner. He kissed it and raised it high in the air.

'Wooooooooooooooooo!' the crowed cheered.

'What a feeling!' he shouted to Iker, who was standing next to him but could barely hear him with the crowd singing and music blaring.

'I know!' Iker called out. 'From Euro 2008 through to tonight, the last six years have been straight out of a fairytale book.'

'Let's hope there are a few more chapters left,' Sergio said, as he waved and blew kisses to the crowd.

CHAPTER 18

EL CAPITÁN

Sergio's life had been a whirlwind over the previous twelve months. He loved every part of it, but it was still exhausting. Pilar and their newborn son Sergio Jr. had turned his world upside down in the best possible way, and even the worst days didn't seem so bad anymore. As part of Spain's squad for the 2014 World Cup in Brazil, Sergio had been gloomy for a day or two when they were eliminated at group stage, but his family quickly had him smiling again. There was more to look forward to as well – Pilar was pregnant with baby number two.

One day, Sergio was sitting in his back garden, enjoying a rare summer break, when his phone buzzed. It was Pérez, the President of Real Madrid.

Sergio answered straight away. 'Hi Florentino. I thought you were on vacation.'

'I am, but I wanted to book a time to meet with you when I'm back. We need to finalise your new contract and I have a few other things to talk through.'

'Sure thing. I'm going to be at the Bernabéu with René next Thursday for a club event, so we can drop by then.'

When Sergio and René sat down in Florentino's office and took a sip of the water laid out for him, Pérez turned suddenly and said, 'Can you believe you've been a Real Madrid player for ten years now?'

'In some ways, it feels like it can't possibly be that long, but then I think about what has happened in my life, on and off the pitch, and I guess it makes sense. I'll always remember how you put your trust in me, even as a teenager.'

'I had a feeling, right from the start, that you were going to be a superstar. Then when you came in and started crunching Ronaldo and Raúl, I knew for sure.'

They all laughed.

'Well, let's start with the contract,' Pérez said, looking at both Sergio and René. 'We see you at the very centre of the next era at Real Madrid. Our offer reflects that. You don't have to sign anything today but see what you think.'

He leaned forward and passed across two folders with documents inside. Sergio and René read through the offer. René had coached Sergio years ago to keep a serious face in these meetings and not give away what he was thinking.

'It's clear that you value Sergio,' René said, closing his folder. 'Just give us a day or two to talk it over and we'll give you a firm answer.'

'Excellent,' Pérez replied. 'There's one other thing I want to cover today that is sort of linked to the contract offer.'

Sergio leaned forward in his seat, eager to hear more.

'Obviously, it was a tough blow to lose Iker to Porto this summer after all his years of service with Real Madrid but now we have to find a new club captain. We need someone who loves Real Madrid, has the respect of all his teammates and is a proven winner. We'd like it to be you.'

Sergio smiled and put his hands to his mouth. 'Wow, what an honour! Real Madrid captain – I like the sound of that.'

Pérez grinned. 'You're a natural leader and you've been setting an example for the boys for years now. It's time for you to take over the armband.'

As Sergio and René headed back to the car, they walked in silence. Once they set off driving, though, Sergio couldn't stay quiet any longer.

'That feeling of walking out at the Bernabéu as captain is going to be incredible,' he said.

'To be fair, it's a great contract offer too,' said René. 'We can take another look through it tonight, but I expect we can give Florentino a quick answer on that too.'

The next morning, Sergio called Florentino to give him the good news: yes and yes.

'Fantástico!' Florentino replied. Sergio could hear him tapping his desk in celebration. 'The next few years are going to be a lot of fun for Real Madrid.'

As Sergio played with Sergio Jr. at the park that afternoon, he was excited to have a few more weeks of family time before getting back into football mode, but equally he couldn't wait for the new era at Real Madrid to start.

CHAPTER 19

MORE SUCCESS WITH ZIZOU

When Sergio heard the news about the new Real Madrid manager, he hopped out of his seat and turned on the TV. It was official now – Zidane, who had worked with the players a lot when Carlo was in charge, was taking over.

'Is the bald guy in charge now?' Pilar asked, grinning.

'That's Zidane!' Sergio shot back. 'You can't call him that! But yes, he's the new boss.'

At training later that week, the new boss called Sergio aside. 'Did you ever think I'd be your manager one day when we were chasing trophies together?' Zizou joked.

Sergio laughed. 'I guess I thought you'd have your feet up at the beach when you retired.'

'I got bored of the quiet life pretty quickly, and I loved working with Carlo and you guys. It made me realise that I wanted to be in the hot seat eventually.'

'Well, this is going to be a fun ride. The boys are all really excited. Some of them had posters of you on their wall growing up.'

Zizou rolled his eyes. 'Thanks for making me feel like an old man!'

They carried on walking around the pitch as the training session continued around them.

'Listen, Sergio, we have a chance to do something really special here. We've got it all – a solid defence, midfield playmakers and deadly strikers. But it all starts with you. The players look up to you. When you talk, they listen. Together, we've got to keep everyone focused but give them the freedom to play the Real Madrid way.'

Sergio nodded. Zizou knew the club inside out and there was already a lot of talk about Real Madrid soon being back to their attacking best.

The consistent league form was still a work in progress that season, but Real Madrid's love affair with the Champions League continued as Zizou guided them back to the 2016 final. Just as in 2014, they would face Atlético. Sergio still got goosebumps when he thought about his last-minute header from two years earlier.

He felt confident as he led the team out for the final, and determined to get the team off to a good start. He never missed a chance to get into the box for corners and free kicks, and he jogged up to join Cristiano and Karim for a first-half set piece. The ball flew into the box through a sea of bodies and landed right at Sergio's feet. He reacted quickest and poked the ball into the net.

Gooooooooooooooooooooaaaaaaaaaaaaaaaaalllllllllllll llllllllllllll!!!!!!!!!!!!!!!!!!!

But Atlético fought back, putting Sergio in the spotlight for yet another penalty shootout. As usual, he was the fourth taker, and he marched forward to pick up the ball and place it on the spot. The shootout was locked at 3–3. He took a moment to steady himself, paused for a split second in his run up to fool the keeper and then stroked the ball into the bottom corner. He pumped his fist in celebration. As the next Atlético penalty bounced back off the post, Sergio was jumping up and down. 'Come on, Cristiano. You've got this!' he called out.

Cristiano made no mistake and Real Madrid were champions again. Sergio threw himself onto the pile of teammates already surrounding Cristiano.

A year later, Zizou was still working his magic. Real Madrid had reclaimed La Liga and were back in the Champions League final again – this time against Juventus. It was another tense first half but Sergio watched from the back in admiration as the Real Madrid midfield took over in the second half.

The highlight of yet another magical European night was a celebration on the pitch at the end, for which Sergio was joined by his family: Pilar, Sergio Jr. and the newest addition, Marco. Even though Sergio was tired and sweaty, there was nothing better than sharing that moment with the people he loved most in the whole world.

Sergio thought back to what Iker had told him years before when Barcelona were the powerhouse of Spanish football. 'Our time will come,' Iker had said.

'I guess this is our time,' Sergio said to himself as the Real Madrid fans sang the players' names again and again.

With Zizou, there was no chance of taking things easy. He made that very clear when the squad arrived for the 2017/18 season. 'We're starting with a clean slate again. The Champions League wins count for nothing, and teams are going to be even more desperate to stop us, especially Barcelona. We can't let it slip now.'

Sergio led by example, demanding even more from his teammates. He had the authority to tell Cristiano to stop sulking, or to tell Luka to get more involved. They had been through so many battles together that the dressing room had a family feel.

Again, Real Madrid proved too strong in the
knockout rounds, reaching a third consecutive
Champions League final. 'There was a time when
I couldn't picture winning even one Champions
League title,' he told Pilar at breakfast the week
before the 2018 final. 'Now, I have a chance to lift
the trophy as captain for a third time.'

Pilar smiled. 'Well, we'll be there to cheer you on.
It's funny, I've been trying to explain to Sergio Jr.
that football isn't usually like this. He expects to see
you in the final every year.'

Like the previous two finals, a familiar pattern
emerged in 2018. Real Madrid scored first, had
lots of the ball then had to regroup after a surprise
equaliser. Liverpool were pressuring them all over
the field and the game was hanging in the balance.
'Keep going, guys,' Sergio called out, clapping his
hands. 'Move the ball, find the open man.'

Luka and Toni took back control in midfield – and
then Zizou made the key change, bringing Gareth
on. Minutes later, Gareth scored one of the best
goals Sergio had ever seen – an unstoppable bicycle

kick into the top corner. Sergio punched the air. They had one hand on the trophy.

When the final whistle finally arrived, it was a familiar scene with Sergio at the centre of the party. 'I love you guys,' he told every teammate he could find. 'Champions again!'

CHAPTER 20

THE ROAD AHEAD

Real Madrid's Champions League winning streak was foiled in the 2018/19 season, and Sergio could tell that another new era was approaching. One by one, his best friends had moved on: Iker had signed for Porto, and then his centre-back partner Pepe had joined Beşiktaş. Now, Cristiano had been sold to Juventus, and Sergio sensed that other players were looking for a new challenge.

After all, what else was there left for him to achieve at Real Madrid? From a raw and reckless nineteen-year-old right-back, he had gone on to become one of the deadliest defenders in the world, winning everything along the way: four La Liga titles, four

Champions League trophies, four FIFA Club World Cups, three UEFA Super Cups and two Spanish Cups.

And that was just at club level; Sergio had also won two European Championships and a World Cup with his country, Spain.

But despite all that success, at the age of thirty-three, Sergio was still learning lessons. He kicked himself for trying to work the Champions League yellow card rules in his favour. By getting booked in the Round of 16 first leg against Ajax, he thought it was a safe bet to miss the second leg and return for the next round. But Ajax stunned the Bernabéu with a 4–1 win as Sergio watched from the crowd. He could hardly believe what he was seeing.

As he looked to the future, Sergio knew there were plenty of options, but all that could wait. He had a summer ahead to enjoy with friends and family, and a chance to reflect on everything he had achieved in his career.

'Whatever comes next, it's sure to be a wild adventure,' Pilar said, putting her arms around him. 'Just follow your heart.'

Sergio smiled. As long as Pilar and the boys were with him, he couldn't go wrong.

With a beautiful red-and-orange sunset in front of him, Sergio turned to Pilar, René and his parents. 'I've been thinking a lot about everything you've all done for me along the way,' he said. 'I'm so thankful.'

René shook his head. 'No, we have to thank you as well. This journey has been so memorable for all of us. The little boy from Camas who signed for Real Madrid and won every trophy for club and country. What a story!'

Turn the page for a sneak preview of
another brilliant football story by
Matt and Tom Oldfield. . .

MODRIĆ

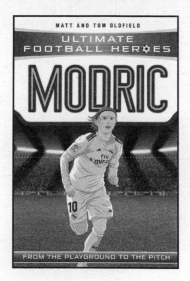

Available now!

CHAPTER 1

CHAMPIONS LEAGUE WINNER

24 May 2014, Estádio da Luz, Lisbon

After nine months of amazing football action, it was time for Europe's biggest match – the Champions League Final!

An incredible 60,000 fans clapped and cheered as the two teams walked out of the tunnel, past the shiny silver trophy, and onto the pitch.

Atleti! Atleti! Atleti!

On one side were Atlético Madrid, wearing their red-and-white stripes. The new Champions of Spain were a very tough team to beat.

Real! Real! Real!

On the other side were their Madrid rivals, the Galácticos, wearing their blue tracksuit tops. The TV cameras moved along their line of superstars:

Ángel Di María, Gareth Bale, Sami Khedira, Raphaël Varane, Karim Benzema, Cristiano Ronaldo…

Tucked in between these footballing giants was Luka, Real Madrid's little midfield maestro. Luka might not have looked that big, but he was as brave as a lion. Alongside Sami, it would be his job to win the ball and pass it forward to Real's fantastic forwards.

'This is our year, lads!' Real's captain Iker Casillas called out before kick-off. 'Let's win *La Décima*!'

The Real Madrid fans had been waiting twelve long years to win their tenth Champions League title. They were getting desperate! But after losing in the semi-finals for three years in a row, their team had, at last, made it all the way to the final once again. Now, they just had to win it.

From the very first minute, Luka controlled the game calmly for Real. It was his first-ever Champions League final but it didn't look that way. What a natural!

Control, turn, perfect pass,
Control, turn, perfect pass,
Control, turn, dribble, then perfect pass!

Luka was always looking to create a goalscoring chance but he never rushed his pass. Patience was key. Eventually, a gap would appear in the Atlético defence.

At five feet eight inches, Luka was one of the smallest players on the pitch, but what did size matter with so much spirit? He made tackles, intercepted passes, and he even won headers!

In the thirty-sixth minute, however, Atlético took the lead. Luka could only watch as Diego Godín's header looped up over Iker's outstretched arm. *1–0!*

'Keep going!' the Real centre-back Sergio Ramos urged his teammates. 'We've got plenty of time to grab an equaliser.'

Luka wasn't the kind of player to panic. He just kept doing what he always did, pushing Real Madrid up the pitch.

Control, turn, perfect pass.
Control, turn, perfect pass.

Control, turn, dribble, then perfect pass!

But as the second half flew by, Real still hadn't scored. Thibaut Courtois saved Cristiano's free kick. Karim shot wide, then Isco, then Gareth.

'How many chances do we need?' Luka groaned, reading the minds of all the anxious Real Madrid supporters in the stands.

When he raced over to take a corner, the match was deep into injury time. It was now or never in the Champions League final...

Luka curled a beautiful cross towards the penalty spot and hoped for the best. There was lots of pushing and shoving in the box but suddenly, Sergio sprang up and headed the ball into the net. *1–1!*

Over by the corner flag, Luka threw his arms up triumphantly. 'We did it!' he roared.

What a goal, and what a time to score it! The Atlético players were distraught; the Real players were delighted. Their *Décima* dream was still alive.

In extra time, Real raced away to victory. Ángel's shot was saved, but Gareth was in the right place to score the rebound. *2–1!*

'Yes!' Luka screamed as he celebrated with his old Tottenham teammate.

This was why they had both moved to Real Madrid – for the glory, for the trophies. When it came to winning, the team was totally ruthless.

Marcelo dribbled forward and shot past Courtois. *3–1!*

Cristiano scored from the penalty spot. *4–1!*

Luka bounced up and down with his brilliant teammates in front of the Real Madrid fans. They were the new Champions of Europe!

After a bad start, it had turned out to be the best night of Luka's life by far. He had a Croatian flag wrapped around his shoulders, a winners' medal around his neck, and soon, he would have the Champions League trophy in his hands!

But first, it was Iker's turn. As the Real Madrid captain lifted the cup high above his head, clouds of white confetti filled the sky. It was time to get the party started.

Campeones, Campeones, Olé! Olé! Olé!

When the trophy finally reached Luka, he held

on tightly. Wow, it was huge, and quite heavy too. Imagine if he dropped it!

'Hurray!' he yelled up into the Lisbon night sky.

It was a moment that Luka would treasure forever. He was a football superstar now. He knew that his grandad would be so proud of him.

CHAPTER 2

GOAT HERDING WITH GRANDAD

'Luka!' a tired voice shouted through the open back door. 'Where are you? I need your help please. We've got work to do.'

'Coming, Grandad!' Luka replied, remembering to grab his coat off the hook before he rushed outside. In winter, it could be bitterly cold on the slopes of the Velebit mountain range where the Modrić family lived.

'Good boy,' his grandad said, giving him a hearty pat on the back. 'Right, let's go.'

As Luka walked beside his grandad, he didn't look up at the wild, lonely landscape that surrounded them. He was used to those views. It was his home, after all. Instead, he kept his head down, looking at the path ahead. He did this for two reasons. The first reason was that the ground was rocky and uneven, and he didn't want to trip and fall. The second reason was that he was searching for the perfect stick.

Luka couldn't herd goats without a good stick – no way! That would be like asking a footballer to play without a football.

'Not bad,' his grandad nodded approvingly when Luka showed him the stick he had chosen. 'That will do nicely.'

Luka was still only five years old but that was old enough to go goat herding with his grandad. Besides, if he didn't help out, who else could? There weren't any kind neighbours nearby; their house was the only house on the street. And Luka's parents, Stipe and Radojka, were too busy working long hours in a local knitwear factory in order to earn money for the family.

So, goat herding was Luka's job and he took it very

seriously. That's why picking the perfect stick was so important.

'No, wrong way!' Luka told any goats that tried to take a different route. He was still very small but he was brave enough to block their path. 'That's it – follow your brothers and sisters!'

It was so peaceful up on the mountain paths. Most of the time, it was just Luka, the goats, and Grandad. What in the world could be better than that? There weren't many other young children in the area, so Grandad was his best friend. As they walked, the old man told lots of exciting stories about his life, and Luka listened carefully, taking in every word.

'But now, the times are changing,' his grandad often warned on their goat-herding adventures together. 'Trouble is on its way.'

Unfortunately, Luka's grandad turned out to be right about that. First came war and sorrow, and then came football and joy.

CHAPTER 3

THE SORROWS OF WAR

On a cold December day in 1991, just a week before Christmas, Luka's grandad led the goats along the mountain slopes as usual. This time, however, he was alone because Luka was busy learning at school. And, sadly, their homeland was no longer a peaceful place.

Their country, Croatia, was fighting fiercely to become an independent nation, separate from Yugoslavia. Yugoslavia, however, weren't going to let them leave without a fight. On that cold December day, soldiers suddenly stormed the village of Modrići, and Luka's grandad was killed.

When he returned from school and heard the

tragic news, Luka was absolutely devastated. He
loved his grandad so much and now they would
never be able to goat herd together again. How could
such a horrible thing happen to his poor, innocent
grandad? War was a very difficult thing for a six-year-
old child to understand.

'I'm so sorry, Luka,' his mum told him tearfully,
'but we have to leave this place straight away. It's not
safe to stay here any longer.'

Their happy days in Modrići were over; now, they
were refugees on the run. The family quickly packed
up their belongings and moved to Zadar, the nearest
city, where Luka and his sister Jasmina had been born.

What now? They had nowhere to live, and they
didn't have enough money to rent a new house of
their own. Fortunately, they were offered a small,
bare room in the Hotel Kolovare. They didn't have
electricity or running water, but at least they had a
shelter from the war.

But even in Zadar, things were far from safe. All
through the day and through the night, Luka and
his family lived with the loud sounds of war. Even

walking out into the streets was a dangerous thing to do. As the fight for independence went on, there was more and more damage everywhere. They were tough and terrible times for the Croatian nation.

'One day, everything will be peaceful again,' Luka's mum promised them as they huddled together to keep warm.

But when? Luka wanted to go back to Modrići. In Zadar, he was only an hour's drive from his old home, but it felt like a lifetime away. It was such a shock to go from the quiet of the countryside to the noise and bustle of a city. Compared to Modrići, Zadar felt really big and scary. There were strange, sad faces everywhere he looked.

'Dad, when are we going back home?' Luka asked again and again.

'We can't, son,' Stipe always replied, his face full of sorrow. 'This is our home now.'

Luka never stopped missing Modrići, the mountains, the goats and most of all, his grandad. But luckily, he found a new love that helped him to escape from the sorrows of war...

SERGIO RAMOS HONOURS

Real Madrid

🏆 La Liga: 2006–07, 2007–08, 2011–12, 2016–17

🏆 Copa del Rey: 2010–11, 2013–14

🏆 Supercopa de España: 2008, 2012, 2017

🏆 UEFA Champions League: 2013–14, 2015–16, 2016–17, 2017–18

🏆 UEFA Super Cup: 2014, 2016, 2017

🏆 FIFA Club World Cup: 2014, 2016, 2017, 2018

Spain

🏆 UEFA European Under-19 Championship: 2004

🏆 UEFA European Championship: 2008, 2012

🏆 FIFA World Cup: 2010

Individual

🏆 La Liga Breakthrough Player of the Year: 2005

🏆 UEFA Team of the Year: 2008, 2012, 2013, 2014, 2015, 2016, 2017, 2018

🏆 FIFA World Cup Dream Team: 2010

🏆 UEFA Euro Team of the Tournament: 2012

🏆 La Liga Best Defender: 2011–12, 2012–13, 2013–14, 2014–15, 2016–17

🏆 UEFA Champions League Squad of the Season: 2013–14, 2015–16, 2016–17, 2017–18

🏆 La Liga Team of the Season: 2015–16

🏆 UEFA Defender of the Season: 2017, 2018

RAMOS

4 **THE FACTS**

NAME: SERGIO RAMOS GARCÍA

DATE OF BIRTH: 30 March 1986

AGE: 33

PLACE OF BIRTH: Camas

NATIONALITY: Spanish

BEST FRIEND: Cristiano Ronaldo

CURRENT CLUB: Real Madrid

POSITION: CB

THE STATS

Height (cm):	**184**
Club appearances:	**682**
Club goals:	**89**
Club trophies:	**20**
International appearances:	**165**
International goals:	**20**
International trophies:	**3**
Ballon d'Ors:	**0**

★ ★ ★ **HERO RATING: 87** ★ ★ ★

GREATEST MOMENTS

1 10 MARCH 2007, BARCELONA 3–3 REAL MADRID

After his €27 million move to Real Madrid, Sergio
soon showed what a big game player he was. In this
El Clásico match at Barcelona's Nou Camp stadium,
he outjumped his Spain teammate Carles Puyol to
score a fantastic flick header. Sergio's goal helped
earn his team an important draw and two months
later, he lifted the first of his four La Liga titles.

29 JUNE 2008, GERMANY 0–1 SPAIN

Sergio played brilliantly as Spain's right-back at Euro 2008. And like all big game players, he saved his best performance for the final, against Germany. He never stopped running all game long, helping his team at both ends of the pitch. At the final whistle, Spain were the new European Champions and that was just the start…

11 JULY 2010, NETHERLANDS 0–1 SPAIN

At the 2010 World Cup in South Africa, Sergio and his Barcelona rivals Carles Puyol and Gerard Piqué only conceded two goals over the entire tournament. And after a hard-fought final against the Netherlands, Spain were crowned the new World Champions. Sergio was also named in the World Cup Dream Team.

24 MAY 2014, REAL MADRID 4–1 ATLÉTICO MADRID

This was Sergio's first Champions League Final, but he didn't let that faze him. With seconds to go, Real Madrid were losing 1–0 to their local rivals, Atlético. Sergio had scored two goals in the semi-final against Bayern Munich, and he scored again in the final to rescue his team. As the cross came in, he rose highest to head the ball down into the bottom corner. 1–1! Real Madrid went on to win 4–1 in extra time, but it was all thanks to Sergio.

21 JUNE 2016, REAL MADRID 1–1 ATLÉTICO MADRID (5–3 ON PENS)

Another Champions League final against Atlético, another goal from Sergio. This time, he gave Real Madrid the lead, and with his foot rather than his head. When the match then went to penalties, Sergio stepped up and coolly scored their fourth spot-kick, before Cristiano Ronaldo blasted home the winner.

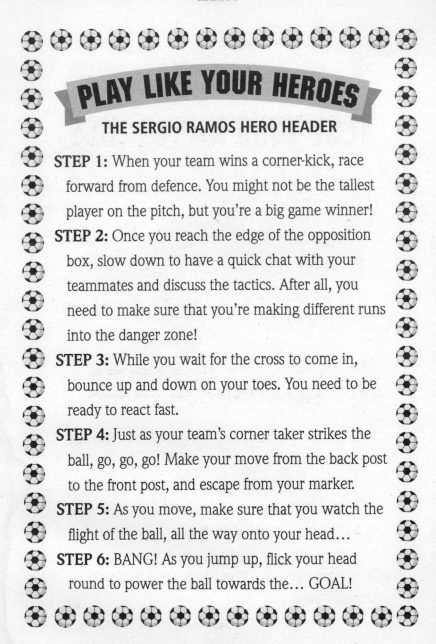

PLAY LIKE YOUR HEROES

THE SERGIO RAMOS HERO HEADER

STEP 1: When your team wins a corner-kick, race forward from defence. You might not be the tallest player on the pitch, but you're a big game winner!

STEP 2: Once you reach the edge of the opposition box, slow down to have a quick chat with your teammates and discuss the tactics. After all, you need to make sure that you're making different runs into the danger zone!

STEP 3: While you wait for the cross to come in, bounce up and down on your toes. You need to be ready to react fast.

STEP 4: Just as your team's corner taker strikes the ball, go, go, go! Make your move from the back post to the front post, and escape from your marker.

STEP 5: As you move, make sure that you watch the flight of the ball, all the way onto your head…

STEP 6: BANG! As you jump up, flick your head round to power the ball towards the… GOAL!

TEST YOUR KNOWLEDGE

QUESTIONS

1. Which football tournament did little Sergio watch Spain win in 1992?

2. What was the name of the boy that Sergio had to pretend to be when he first joined Camas Juniors?

3. Which Spanish club scouted Sergio when he was ten years old?

4. How old was Sergio when he made his La Liga debut and in what position did he play?

5. Which manager first called Sergio up to the Spain national team?

6. How much money did Real Madrid pay to sign Sergio in 2005?

7. Who was the manager of Spain when Sergio and co won the World Cup in 2010?

8. What happened to Sergio in the 2012 Champions League semi-final?

9. Who did Sergio replace as Real Madrid captain in 2015?

10. How many World Cups has Sergio played at and how many goals has he scored?

11. How many goals has Sergio scored in Champions League finals, excluding penalties?

Answers below. . . No cheating!